Baking

with passion

Baker & Spice

Baking

with passion

exceptional recipes for real breads, cakes, and pastries

Dan Lepard and Richard Whittington

special photography by Peter Williams

THUNDER BAY
P·R·E·S·S

San Diego, California

to Karen Copland and Barry Stephens

Thunder Bay Press
An imprint of the Advantage Publishers Group
5880 Oberlin Drive, San Diego, CA 92121-4794
www.advantagebooksonline.com

Text © Richard Whittington and Dan Lepard
Recipe photography © Peter Williams
Location photography © Emily Andersen
Design and layout © Quadrille Publishing Ltd

All notations of errors or omissions should be addressed to Thunder
Bay Press, editorial department, at the above address. All other corre-
spondence (author inquiries, permissions) concerning the content of
this book should be addressed to Quadrille Publishing Limited,
Alhambra House, 27-31 Charing Cross Road, London
WC2H 0LS, England.

ISBN 1-57145-829-8

Library of Congress Cataloging-in-Publication Data available upon
request.

Printed in China.

1 2 3 4 5 06 05 04 03 02

Contents

Introducing
Baker & Spice

"I think bread is special, something simple and honest yet delicious. Every time you break it, smell it, eat it, it makes life a little better, even if it is only for 5 minutes. Good bread is something you never get bored with. It delights afresh, every day. In essence, it describes both who we are at Baker & Spice and why we are." GAIL STEPHENS

Baker & Spice was not an idea that sprang fully formed into Gail Stephens' mind. Her most extraordinary and beautiful shop that sits so prettily in smart Walton Street in London started its life as a window for her existing trade-baking business. It was only gradually, as the Victorian ovens were restarted and on-site production began for the local community, that it took shape and flourished, developing the unique identity that has made it famous.

When you visit the shop the first impressions are overwhelming. This is the bakery and pâtissierie of your dreams, and those dreams were probably set in Paris, not London. As you admire the stacks of beautiful breads and trays of captivating pastries giving off their sweet, alluring smells—all of them handmade by bakers working on the premises and using traditional ingredients and methods—it is hard to believe that the roots of such excellence were in vans, not stone ovens, in a delivery service for bread baked by other people, for customers too small for the big bakers to be bothered with. Today's most shining star in British artisanal baking has its roots in an innovative and successful service operation. With its sound business administration providing financial independence, it allowed Gail Stephens to set the shop up in a way that was thought by many to be commercially untenable in today's marketplace.

"The way the shop is run is really based on how we trade," she says, explaining that the raw ingredients define an attitude as well as a style of food. "I have always been concerned about the provenance as well as the quality of the ingredients we work with. I have never bought solely on price and was warned that my ethical concerns would bankrupt me. The irony is that today the business is very successful.

"We are what we buy, and that has moral as well as price consequences. We use as much that is organic as possible. We work with the seasons and are very careful about where our raw materials come from. Does it have to travel halfway around the world to get to Walton Street? If something comes from the Third World, who exploited whom to get it here? I don't sit in the office and buy blind on the telephone. I go to Covent Garden four times a week, and read and check every label on every box of fresh produce that I buy. I smell and feel the goods as well as taste them. Once a month I go to a big dried fruit, nut, and spice importer. Buying is never on autopilot. I really spend a lot of time with suppliers to get it right.

"We bake things that people respond to in a dramatic way because everything we sell is baked on the premises. What you see is what you get, and what you get is what we make. And that involves learned technique and very hard work. The whole point of Baker & Spice is that it is self-contained; we don't buy in anything ready-made. We do things the way people used to do them, which in the age of intensive farming and the supermarket have largely been forgotten or deliberately ignored. Every day has its own identity. The life span of the product and the way it is produced is just that—a day—and then everything starts from scratch again. Practically, that means seven 18-hour working days in every week.

"Changes occur in what is baked in some sense by natural progression, but also by listening to the customers. Partly because of that we have become a real village shop. We are the neighborhood. We reflect it and it reflects us."

Baker & Spice is remarkable in its consistent delivery, but this is the direct consequence of the caliber of the staff Gail Stephens has brought together over a three-year period. This is not an anonymous place, and the people who work here are encouraged to have an identity as a part of a team whose members inevitably change with time, but who share the same commitment to quality achieved in an ethical environment.

This is not like a restaurant where front of house and back of house function autonomously and often with ill-concealed animosity. Here the two are clearly, happily, and inextricably intertwined. They work together and you cannot see the join, because the service is a seamless process from the cooking to the customer. Indeed, one of the shop's more unusual aspects is in the direct communication between those who cook at the back with the customers, sometimes even serving them. As freshly baked loaves are brought through or another beautiful cake is displayed, it is discussed and commented on. Regulars travel miles for their morning croissant, often in the summer eating it still warm at one of the small tables on the sidewalk in front of the shop.

"The achievement of quality in what we sell is only part of the relationship that connects the individual customer to the process at the back of the shop, where what they buy is made," says Karen Copland, the shop manager. "The shop has to work from the front to the back and from the back to the front. It is important that the people who cook the food don't feel separated from the selling of it. They come in and out of the shop, and they talk to the customers. This is how we all feel it should be."

The bakery

Underneath the street level in Walton Street are two brick ovens, each with the original stone-covered baking floor covering 12 square yards. The ovens were built and installed in 1902, by Robert Hannington and W.H. Young & Co., both London-based companies with excellent reputations. Originally fueled by coal, the steam-generating ovens also provided hot water for the bakery. The steam in a professional oven helps to develop the crust and gives a wonderful bronze color to the bread.

During the 1950s, the ovens were oil-fired, the fuel being piped from outside tanks to the burners that ran around the circumference of the oven. The smoke and excess steam would be carried through a twisting tunnel to the chimney, where it would escape to make its stinking contribution to the smogs that polluted London's air until the Clean Air Act was introduced in 1957.

When Gail Stephens took over the property from Justin de Blank, these ovens were still in use, by then fired by gas. After minor renovations and the addition of a steam-injection system, the ovens were ready to bake bread once again.

Traditionally, breads are put into the oven on heavily floured "peels," which are flat beechwood heads attached to long shafts. Nobody makes these peels in Britain, so they had to be imported from France. Another investment was a double-sized "parisienne," a cupboard used to protect the dough as it rests on unbleached linen sheets. Dozens of cloth-lined reed baskets, in which the big sourdoughs sit during their long fermentation, help to shape the loaves as they rise, and these again had to be sourced from France. For breads requiring a long, chilled rest over many hours, a temperature-controlled "retarder-prover" that could hold over 200 small loaves was installed.

An Artofex mixer capable of working two sacks of flour at a time was also introduced, a British machine invented to replicate the hand-kneading of doughs in wooden troughs, which was the standard practice in bakeries for hundreds of years. This superior and expensive mixer is popular in France and is today mainly sold there. Its unique configuration helps to give the bread an irregular aeration—different-sized bubbles of air throughout the crumb—and its gentle, slow mixing helps to develop the gluten strands.

The breads

Apparently similar constructions of flour, water, and yeast can deliver very different textures and complex, deep flavors. Wheat flours, from the darkest, moist whole-wheat to cream-colored, soft milled flour, rye flours, grains of corn, rice, and malted wheat berries are selected from traditional mills in England, France, and Ireland for Baker & Spice breads. In all, more than a dozen different types of flour, much of it organic and stoneground, are mixed together in different proportions to create individual bread recipes. The blending of flours is a key to creating the "wild-yeast" levains and poolishes that raise doughs naturally, and which contribute significantly to the complex, slightly sour flavor of the finished breads. This is the application of learned practice, essentially artisanal skills that impose consistency on the loaves. There are no chemicals or genetically modified soy improvers to speed things up or make things easier, just the passionate application of knowledge and sheer hard work.

New breads are developed by imagining the finished loaf and then carefully constructing the mix of flours, liquids, leavening materials, and techniques. Each bread is created with its own mix of sour starters or fresh active yeast, flours, grains, and, in some recipes, fruit and fruit juices, vegetables, nuts, fresh herbs, and oils. The sourdoughs are based on four different wild yeast cultures, selected for their proven ability to create healthy, vigorous starters. These vary in moisture content and flour type, and are cared for by regular refreshment and vigorous aeration, activity that in the bakery occurs at programmed intervals throughout each 24-hour period.

The bakery works 18 hours a day, seven days a week, from 10pm until about 7am the next morning, and then from 10am until 6 or 7pm. As many of the processes involved in making the breads take days, each baker will have a hand in the production of every single loaf of bread produced. As an example, the Boule de Meule, a traditional French whole-wheat sourdough, will have been mixed early one morning, developed and shaped during the day, rested for 12 hours, and finally baked very early the next day.

The skills that each member of the baking team brings to the process are capable of wider application since, unusually for a professional baker in Britain, many of the breads are made in small batches, as are the cakes, cookies, and pastries. So the techniques used and the quantities of what is being produced are on a scale much closer to domestic cooking than is typical.

The cakes

There is a tradition of thoughtful cake-making—the skillful mixing of fine ingredients in a bowl, combined by hand, and baked in small batches—which has found continued professional expression at Baker & Spice. It is honest food representing the very best home baking from around the world.

Mass-produced cakes tend to be very basic, but are dressed up after they are baked to make them look more special than they really are. This is quite the opposite of the Baker & Spice approach, where there is little or no decoration of the cakes after they cool from the oven. Here everything is in the making. Thus the final flavor in every Apple and Calvados cake is achieved before the cakes are baked. There is no icing to camouflage and no decoration to distract from poor texture and flavor. What is achieved is the result of the best ingredients and careful baking techniques, nothing more and nothing less.

The pastries and brioches

"Viennoiserie" describes the highly specialized area of croissant and puff pastry-making, something in which Baker & Spice excels. Patrick Lozach was the man who first created the croissants, the brioche, and fine butter pastries for the shop. Trained in Brittany, France, over 20 years ago, his work reflects the traditions of "old school" French baking, before the additives and colors of the chemical industry took hold of the small pâtisseries. As with the bread at Baker & Spice, the source of the ingredients for the *Viennoiserie* plays an important part in the quality Patrick was able to achieve. The doughs are mixed using French "T550," a slow-milled low-extraction wheat flour that gives a crisp texture to the exterior of the croissants and to baguettes. The flour's low gluten content holds the layers intact and separate, through repeated turning and folding, creating a tender, melting crumb and a crisp, short finish to the crust.

Much of the cheaper *Viennoiserie* sold in Britain, and increasingly in France, contains an orange-dyed butter, a mixture of milk fat from E.C. countries, reprocessed and packaged as "French butter." The croissants at Baker & Spice are made exclusively with L'Escure, an *appellation controllé* unsalted French butter. L'Escure is not used because it is from France, but because it is the best butter there is. The pain au chocolat is filled with Belgian Callibaut Couverture—a fine high-cocoa-content chocolate with a strong bittersweet taste. The almond croissants are filled with ground almonds, sugar, butter, and egg yolks. No artificial flavors, no extracts, no bulking agents, just lots of almonds and fresh butter.

Baking with passion encapsulates all the skills of the bakers at Baker & Spice in recipes that, while detailed, communicate simply and logically how to get the best results. Everything is explained, from the consequences of using different yeasts to the impact of working with different flours. You will learn how to replicate the steam-injection used in the bakery to achieve crusted loaves with a delightful chewy crumb. You will discover that working with wetter doughs delivers better bread, and that techniques for gentle kneading and turning improve aeration and texture. All the recipes have been tested in a domestic kitchen using non-professional electric and gas ovens.

Everything that is done in the bakery to maximize the efficiency of production carries through usefully into the practice of the domestic baker. Whether creating tangy sourdough breads with wild yeast starters or learning how to layer pastry with air and butter to produce beautifully crisp and light mille feuilles, this is the most practical of kitchen handbooks. It is not about the hard work of a professional baker, but a story of finding and giving pleasure through the making of delicious things for everyday enjoyment at home.

Essentials

Breadmaking has traditionally been a separate activity within bakeries that also produce cakes, pastries, and cookies, demanding very different skills and time frames. This is the case at Baker & Spice, where different teams work in each area. But the bringing together in the shop of everything that is made expresses the totality of baking as a specialized cooking discipline and, in the range of techniques, tastes, and textures on display, a happy reflection of the home baking experience. If bread is the staff of life, then cakes, pastries, and cookies are part of baking's pleasure principle.

OUR DAILY BREAD

Good bread is a beautiful thing. It is a joy to look at and always a pleasure to eat. Good bread never cloys and we never grow bored with it. Bread is as honest and basic as it is emblematic and significant. Just as rice symbolizes life in the East, and no meal is considered complete without it, so bread is at the very heart of Western civilization. Give us this day our daily bread.

The smell of freshly baked bread, its crackling-crisp crust, its texture when it is broken or sliced, and the consistency of its interior crumb, make it an immensely satisfying and complex culinary assembly. Yet its constituent parts are no more than flour, water, and yeast tempered with a small amount of salt. As you bite into a piece of good baguette you experience all these elements in a taste that combines an underlying sweetness from the wheat, an almost imperceptible balancing sourness from the yeast, and a stronger, contrasting, slightly bitter note from the caramelized crust, the whole drawn together and given depth by the salt.

A sourdough brings different and much stronger flavors, its defining characteristic the acid tang that comes from its lengthy, natural leavening with wild yeasts, the texture altogether denser, more robust, and substantial. This is the darker-colored country bread of ancient tradition, moister, more chewy, and longer lasting, a description that in contemporary usage implies chemical additives but here means the product of its entirely natural development. Such rustic loaves were originally baked in huge ovals, family bread to last a week, changing in taste and texture with progressive cutting and aging, yet taking days before staling. Even when too tough to chew, it may be eaten in soups, or crumbed to add texture or to thicken a variety of dishes. This is indeed bread as the staff of life.

Baking great bread does have a kind of alchemy, for in its artisanal production there are always elements that are beyond technique, though not beyond technical comprehension. Ambient factors play important roles but are not beyond the wit of any competent cook to understand and harness. Even when the same recipe is used, the resulting bread will vary from place to place, as different flours, the water used, temperature, humidity, and even air pressure impact in different ways. Individual technique also plays a part, all these things contributing to the unique quality of the finished loaf.

Excellent bread is not only baked by master bakers. It can be made successfully at home and in standard domestic ovens. The specialist's oven frequently incorporates controllable steam-injection, and it is this steam that helps to form a perfect crust while preventing that crust from being impossibly hard. Most of the breads that we tend to regard as the exclusive preserve of the professional, such as baguettes and sourdoughs, or loaves baked in direct contact with the stone floor of a cavernous bread oven, can in fact be produced in any oven capable of high heat and using a baking stone, steam being generated by spraying water from a bottle.

As with any area of cooking expertise, great bakers have a vocation, and part of it is the ability to communicate how to achieve good and consistent results and to help others find pleasure in the processes of bread's creation. This book is about how to bake good bread at home. With practice, it can become great bread that changes the quality of any and every meal for the better.

FLOUR

Without good flour there can be no good bread. Skill alone cannot achieve it. Flour may be defined as the finely ground meal of any edible grain, though a reasonable assumption today is that it will probably be made from wheat, a description of such vast generalization, perhaps it obscures more than it clarifies. What makes one flour good or appropriate for a given task may make it unsuitable for another. A bag of self-rising flour, with chemical improvers and leavening agents, is unquestionably a white wheat flour, but it is not the stuff from which a good loaf can be made. It may, however, conversely and perversely, be used to bake a decent cake and perhaps a reasonable soda bread.

The history of baking is at least 6,000 years old, though what was called bread at different periods during that time has varied hugely, from the earliest coarse-textured flat cakes cooked on a griddle over an open fire to the airy complexity of today's perfect baguette baked in a steam-injected oven. Wheat is capable of being ground more finely than most other grains, a fact that has always been identified with privilege. The bread of the poor for thousands of years was grim, coarse stuff of millet, oats, barley, and rye, perceived by those with higher standards of living as a damning card of social identity. In hard times, virtually anything might bulk the breads of poverty, including dried legumes, chestnuts, weeds, and—when starvation loomed—sawdust and even clay.

As the superiority of wheat over other grains reflected social hierarchies, so its finest expression was seen to be an ever more refined flour, with less and less husk and wheat germ left in. The whiter and finer the bread, the higher up the social ladder the eater was perceived to be. It is only in the last 100 years that the beneficial role the bits sifted out and discarded to achieve this cosmetic enhancement might play in diet and digestion has been recognized, leading to today's rapidly expanding market for breads that add value by deliberately including bran from the husk, nutty-tasting wheat germ, and other grains and seeds. From a nutritional point of view, such "wholegrain" loaves are not intrinsically better for you, unless your daily diet is completely deficient in B vitamins and fiber. Choice today between white or brown, chewy or finely textured, is really only a matter of taste.

A typical grain of wheat is $\frac{1}{4}$-inch long and $\frac{1}{8}$-inch thick. It is made up of a multilayered cellulose husk—the bran—which surrounds a hard center, 20 percent of which is the oily and vitamin-rich wheat germ—the embryo from which it germinates—the rest being the starchy endosperm. This contains all the gluten-forming proteins that the embryo consumes as it starts to grow. Millers begin by selecting and buying a number of different wheat varieties to create a mix that they can reproduce consistently. Infrared analysis determines key characteristics, including protein content and humidity levels. Cleaning involves brushing and the use of magnets to remove metal contamination prior to washing and drying before milling.

Since industrial roller technology was first developed in the 1830s by the Swiss, most flours have been steel-ground, a high-speed process that generates heat from friction and that damages various aspects of the flour, including the gluten level and the vitamins and enzymes found in the wheat germ. Roller milling passes cleaned wheat grains between a succession of ribbed steel rollers rotating at high speed in opposite directions, the bran and germ being separated and sifted out, leaving behind only the whiter flour derived from the endosperm. This is ground finer and finer with progressive sifting between each grinding—known technically as bolting—

until an ivory-colored and powdery flour results. The extraction of the oily wheat germ means the flour keeps better, but the flavor is less pronounced. Once milled and stored, flour bleaches naturally with time, but storing is expensive, so this whitening is now usually achieved rapidly with chlorine gas. After this the flour may have tiny amounts of niacin, riboflavin, thiamin, and iron added to compensate for the vitamins and minerals lost during steel grinding.

The ancient practice of grinding wheat between slowly turning stones, which has gone on uninterrupted for thousands of years—at first powered by hand, later by water mills, and today by electricity—is once again becoming more common. As a more discerning market continues to develop, so higher quality stoneground flours, once only available to the baking trade or at retail through healthfood stores, are to be found in better supermarkets. Yet this remains a fledgling business when compared to France, where some 2,500 independent small mills operate—in Britain there are perhaps 25. The most significant difference between French and British flours is that the former are milled at a slower speed, resulting in flours that retain more of the wheat's gluten. British bakers tend to achieve higher gluten flours for breadmaking by adding harder imported Canadian flours to the bulk of home-grown flours, an expensive practice because of high import tariffs. The higher the protein level, the less bran the flour will contain.

White flours not described as for bread are low in gluten, in other words "soft." As a general rule, flours for making bread are harder, the hardest containing as much as 14 percent of the total weight as gluten-forming proteins. Some breadmaking flours, like the French T550 used for baguettes, are quite soft but have other important qualities, including a low water-absorbing quotient, that make them ideal for this application. Soft flours are mostly used with

chemical leavening agents in wet batters for making cakes or to make pastries. Flour described as self-rising includes baking powder and other "improvers." Improver is the trade name for any chemical added to a flour to accentuate a given characteristic, for example to slow staling or to encourage and accelerate a particular process such as yeast activation. These are the standard tools of industrial baking, but have no valid role to play in the artisanal or home baker's breadmaking.

So-called whole-wheat flours are darker in color because they are made using the whole grain or the endosperm plus some of the wheat germ and husk. The precise percentages determine how dark and strong tasting the flour will be. Whole-wheat flours consequently have a nuttier taste, which is imparted by the oily wheat germ. The inclusion of wheat germ and bran affects more than taste and texture, as they also impact on the gluten action and result in a lower rise and a denser loaf.

With French flours, the T numeral is a designation describing the degree of sifting from whole grain, from the coarsest whole-wheat to the finest white. The T stands for *taux des cendres*, the ash level left behind after a flour has been incinerated in a laboratory at 900°C. The greater the amount of ash, the higher the level of bran in the flour. Thus the T550 of baguette flour indicates that 55 milligrams of ash is left after burning 100 grams of standard white flour.

TYPES OF FLOUR USED AT BAKER & SPICE

T450 This is a soft, fine French flour, which we use for most of our cakes and cookies.
T550 French white baguette flour, this is finely ground and soft, but with a low moisture absorbency level.
"00" ITALIAN FLOUR Unlike the carefully regulated French T designations, the description of "OO" applied to Italian flour is not an absolute description of a protein level. As a general rule it describes a

relatively hard flour, typically used for making pasta and breads, but different millers will produce flours of varying degrees of hardness.
DOVES FARM ORGANIC WHITE BREAD FLOUR This is a classic stoneground white flour from Hungerford, England.
CHURCHILL WHITE BREAD FLOUR This is similar to Doves Farm.
ODLUM'S IRISH CREAM FLOUR A white self-riser, this is the best flour we have come across for soda bread and scones. We also use it when making cakes.
FARINE DE MEULE (T850) This is a French light whole-wheat, pinkish in color with no discernible flecks of bran.
FARINE DE MEULE (T1100) 100 percent whole-wheat, this French flour includes all the husk and germ.
GRANARY FLOUR A British 100 percent whole-wheat, this has whole malted wheat and barley grains.
ORGANIC WHOLEMEAL FLOUR This is an English whole-wheat flour with 100 percent of the grain.
CAMPAILLOU Developed in France in 1970, this includes malt and dried levain to give a slightly sour flavor; it also includes the yeast catalyst amyl amylase.
FARINE DE SEIGLE A French 100 percent rye flour, this is dark and with a strong and distinctive taste. Its inclusion in a loaf changes the color appreciably, while the chemical make-up of the rye grain inhibits gluten action in the wheat flour with which it is mixed, thus producing a denser texture.

NOTES FOR THE COOK

• In the recipes, measurements are given in cups and spoons as well as in metric weights. The two sets of measurements are not exact conversions.

• All recipes use large eggs, which we have assumed weigh on average 2 ounces each.

• The salt of choice in this book is Maldon, the best flake sea salt in the world. To assist its even distribution throughout a dough or batter, it needs to be blitzed in a food processor to give a uniform, fine grind.

• The amount of flour needed for a bread dough can vary, depending on the flour itself and the heat and humidity in the kitchen. You may need a little more or a little less flour than a recipe specifies, so when trying a recipe for the first time, add most of the flour, reserving the rest to add if needed.

• The use of bottled, still spring water is specified for our bread recipes. This does not rule out the use of tap water, but bottled water is less likely to contain chlorine or other chemicals that may impede yeast activity. This is particularly important with wild yeasts, which are sensitive to even very low concentrations of chemicals. Organic ingredients are recommended for the same reason. The less contaminated a water and flour starter environment, the faster and more aggressively the airborne yeasts will culture and work.

• For recipes that are leavened with active yeast, we always use fresh yeast in the bakery, but in adapting recipes for this book we have opted for instant or quick-rising active dry yeast instead. If you wish to use fresh yeast, a package (1 scant tablespoon) of quick-rising active dry yeast is the equivalent of one cake (0.6-ounce) of compressed fresh yeast.

• The temperature at which you add water to a bread dough must be determined by the relative temperatures of the other elements involved. Thus, if you keep your flour in a cold place and the bowl of the mixer is cold, you need to compensate by making the water hotter and by warming the mixing bowl. Aim for a dough temperature of 72–75°F. Whether your kitchen is cold or hot will also make a difference.

• Ambient temperature is a key determining feature in yeast activity. While yeasts work at temperatures as low as 37°F, the majority of doughs are risen at temperatures that maximize fermentation. When a very warm environment is called for, somewhere with a typical temperature of 82–86°F is ideal. All other times, a "warm place" means a temperature around 68–73°F, draft-free. Where specific temperatures are required, this is always given in the recipes.

• When sufficiently baked, any loaf will have lost a lot of moisture. While with experience you can tell by smell, feel, and appearance when a loaf is properly cooked, a practical test is to weigh it before it goes in the oven. When you think it is done, weigh it straight from the oven. If ready the loaf should be 20 percent lighter than when it went in.

OVENS AND EQUIPMENT

All the recipes in this book have been tested in standard but contemporary gas and electric ovens without convection. Before starting to bake, it's a good idea to invest in an oven themometer to check your oven's temperature variations and its maximum temperature. You may be in for an unpleasant surprise.

Even brand new and expensive ovens carry no guarantees that they will achieve the 500°F you really need for at least the initial baking of many breads. If your oven is some degrees below this, you need to have the problem investigated. Usually the cause is a faulty thermostat, or the oven may have been wrongly calibrated. If the oven is new, you should have no difficulty in having the problem rectified.

A more difficult problem to overcome with an underperforming gas oven is gas pressure. Your gas supplier should be contacted if this turns out to be the cause of an oven not achieving high temperatures.

Gas pressure may also drop if the in-house gas distribution is linked to other appliances, such as the boiler.

As all keen cooks know, you never seem to have too much cooking equipment and there is always a use for another bowl, whisk, or sieve. Measuring by weight is much more accurate than measuring by volume, so kitchen scales are a must for the serious baker. A powerful electric mixer is another great asset. Bread flours demand strong and lengthy kneading, which is hard work done by hand.

Wherever possible, we have suggested the minimum rather than the maximum requirements. Thus, instead of the wooden peel used by bakers to slide bread into the oven, we suggest using a rimless metal cookie sheet. A spray bottle or plant mister will provide you with a steam-generating capability, but be sure to give it a cycle in the dishwasher if it was previously filled with a cleaning product.

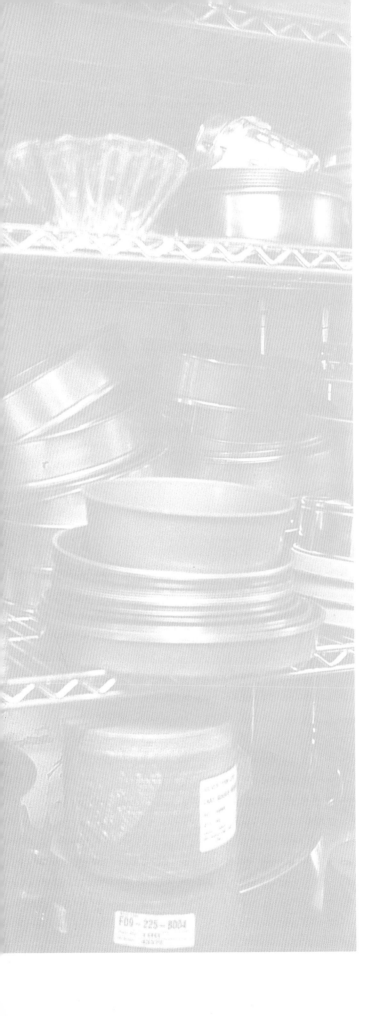

MUST HAVES:

measuring cups and spoons

scales—digital is best

heavy-duty electric mixer with dough hook, mixing paddle,
    and whisk attachments

balloon whisks

food processor

selection of mixing bowls in different sizes

plastic containers for levains and poolishes (2-quart with lids)

wooden spoons, numerous

wooden board for shaping

metal dough scraper

plastic and rubber spatulas

metal spatula

scissors

rolling pin

rimless metal cookie sheet (for peel)

linen cloths and dish towels

oven thermometer

several heavy baking sheets

nonstick jellyroll pans

loaf pans, 1 pound (8$\frac{1}{2}$ x 4$\frac{1}{2}$ x 2$\frac{1}{2}$-inch) and 2 pound
    (10 x 5 x 3-inch)

cake pans in different sizes, both round and square

springform pans in different sizes

tart pans with removable bottoms (large and individual)

pastry bag and tips

pastry cutters

steel ruler

nonstick baking liner or parchment paper

razor blade

pastry brush

water spray bottle or plant mister

skewer for testing cakes

wire cooling rack

OPTIONAL, BUT HELPFUL:

calculator

digital timer

flour bench brush

flour dredger

linen-lined baskets for rising

baking stone

deep-frying/candy thermometer—digital is best

marble slab

large and small brioche molds

English muffin rings

HANDLING BREAD DOUGHS

The way you handle any bread dough will determine how easily you control its shaping and development. It will also affect the rise and, ultimately, the baked texture. You should never be aggressive, which is why the standard description "punch down" is not used, since it implies a rather belligerent treatment. We encourage a more gentle approach, which pays dividends in improved elasticity by encouraging the formation of better distributed gluten strands and a better crumb in the loaf.

Making a soft dough

Many Baker & Spice breads are the product of very wet doughs, difficult to work with and untypical in most baking. They are too sticky to knead successfully by hand and can put an intolerable strain on the motors of heavy-duty electric mixers. We have found, however, that by repeated but minimal kneading during an extended fermentation process, you can aerate and develop the dough with little effort and to remarkable effect.

Essentially, we use repeated gentle deflations of the dough during the initial rise, something described in French as *donner le tour* (to give a turn). To make life easier, we use some flour or olive oil so that you don't stick yourself to the dough. Each of the "turns" lightly stretches the dough, as the yeast continues to work on the strands of gluten. By the last "turn" we are left with a soft, satin-like dough, free of any flour lumps and elastic to the touch.

MIXING THE DOUGH
Place the dry ingredients in a large bowl and add the yeast liquid first, then whatever other ingredients the recipe calls for. Stir with your hands until the mixture forms a rough ball in the center of the bowl (1, 2, 3). At first you will think the mixture is too wet and sticky, but don't worry—it is supposed to be. It's the high water content that helps to give the bread its holes.

THEN, IF THE RECIPE CALLS FOR OIL

Tip a little oil on top of the dough and rub a little on your hands before starting to tuck the dough underneath itself (1). Rotate the bowl, not the dough, and each time you do, continue tucking the dough under with your fingertips until the mass feels smoother on top (2). Cover the bowl with plastic wrap and let rise in a warm place for 45 minutes, or according to the recipe instructions. Repeat to make a satiny dough (3, 4, 5).

OR, IF THE RECIPE USES NO OIL

Cover the work surface lightly with flour. Tip the dough onto the flour, and dust the top and your hands with more flour. Now begin to tap the dough out firmly with the palm and heel of your hand until it forms a rectangle about 2 inches thick. The precise size will obviously depend on the quantities in the recipe you are working from.

With the heel of your hand, pin out the dough into a rough rectangle. Fold it in half (1), then into three the other direction,

until the dough is folded like a blanket (2, 3). Dust the bowl with flour and return the dough to it. Cover and let rise in a warm place for 45 minutes, or according to the recipe instructions.

Whether using the oil or flour method, repeat the action as recommended in the recipe for the duration of the fermentation. By the end you will have a lively, soft, and lump-free dough.

Kneading
a firm dough

Kneading is not an art, but a skill that can be learned. When you watch a professional baker you will be astonished by the speed at which he works and impressed by the economy of his movements. A baker has to work fast because even in artisanal bakeries the output is staggering. Speed is not an affectation or showing off but a necessity, for without speed and focused energy the loaves would not be in the shop on time or in sufficient numbers for the customers to buy. Working in a domestic context the emphasis is not on speed—you are only going to be making a few loaves at a time— but on the kneading, and you will soon get the feeling for that. When you discover how delicious your own bread is and how little effort it takes to produce, this ceases to be a one-off exercise and you become a regular baker. Repetition and practice make for consistency in what you produce and the effort and time involved decrease. The only magic needed to create the same silky-smooth dough as a professional baker is a strong but light touch and an awareness of critical stage changes in the dough as you work it.

During the kneading, you change the structure of the dough with your hands, helping to create a uniform mixture, developing and distributing the gluten strands while stimulating the yeasts. Understanding the consequences of what you are doing and why you are doing it will help you to develop the perfect method to get great results every time.

SOME BASIC RULES:

• Work quickly and on a wooden work surface if possible.
• Keep your work surface clean and dry, covered only by the lightest dusting of flour.
• Keep your hands clean and free from sticky lumps of dough.
• Dust flour on the work surface and your hands, and only on the dough if necessary.

• Be light but firm, not heavy-handed. Dough is tough and resilient and you must dominate it, not the other way around.

THE METHOD

Lightly dust the work surface with flour, and dust your hands. Tip the rough mass of dough onto the surface, then start to fold it into the center (1). As you fold each corner in, press it down with the heel of your hand. Rotate the dough a quarter turn, then repeat the process, until all of the rough edges have been folded in (2).

Fold the dough over in half toward you, stopping it flipping back with your thumb (3). With the heel of your hand, press smoothly and gently into the mass, lifting your thumb away and turning the dough by a quarter in the same fluid movement. Do this again, concentrating on the process, the fluidity, the rhythm. Forget about the world for 10 minutes. Just concentrate on folding, pressing down and across with the heel of

your hand, turning the dough by a quarter, then repeating the action over and over. The texture will change and the dough will become sticky. Then you'll need to scatter some more flour onto the surface and to dust your hands. How often you do this is not something you can write down. It comes from the feel of the dough in your fingertips.

While kneading, break off from time to time to keep the work surface clean, using a scraper to remove any lumps of dough. Add a little flour as you need to—only to the surface under the dough and to your hands. Experience will tell you how often you need to do this. Eventually the dough will become beautifully smooth and elastic (4).

Shaping loaves

It sounds paradoxical, but there is more to shaping doughs than giving the raw dough an approximate shape which suggests that of the finished loaf. Different techniques are used to achieve different shapes, with the preliminary kneading and folding contributing to the final baked form.

A ROUND LOAF

Tip the dough onto a lightly floured work surface. Lightly flatten with your fingertips, then fold an edge of the dough into the center and press it down firmly. Rotate the dough 20° counterclockwise, and repeat the folding and pressing action with another edge of the dough. Continue rotating and folding until all of the edges have been folded into the center.

Next, flip the ball of dough over so that the smooth underside is facing up. Gripping your hands around the dough, drag and turn the ball firmly across the work surface. Then pick the dough up, return it to its starting place, and repeat the action a few more times. This compacts the dough and helps the strands of gluten align—which in turn helps the bread to rise dramatically in the oven during baking.

A BAGUETTE

Place the dough on a lightly floured work surface. (Too much flour on the work surface will hinder rather than help you.) Flour your hands. Tap the dough out with your hands to flatten it slightly. Fold the top edge of the dough to the center and fold the bottom edge up to meet it. Press down with your fingertips (1). Starting at one end, and in a continuous movement, roll the dough over toward you while closing the seam with the fingertips of your other hand as you work your way along its length (2). Repeat this action two or three times until you have a seamless, sausage-shaped coherent mass.

Finish by rolling the loaf with the palms of your hands, moving them from the center of the loaf outward (3), to encourage an even narrowing and lengthening of the shape (4).

A BÂTON

Tip the dough onto a floured work surface and lightly knead into a ball. Tap out with your hands to form a rectangle. Fold the upper edge of the dough toward the center. Press it down with your fingertips. Then fold the right and left ends of the dough in by $^3/_4$ inch, slightly on an angle so that the dough is vaguely triangular (1). Press these ends firmly to seal. Now fold the upper edge of the dough over to meet the lower edge, and seal it down firmly with your fingers (2). Finally, flip the dough around, so that the ends are reversed, and once more fold the upper edge over to meet the lower edge, sealing it down with the heel of your hand (3). Flip the shaped dough over so the seam is on top (4).

Shaping rolls

Rolls can be shaped from virtually any dough, though ours are typically based on pain blanc (page 52), delivering a nice, crisp crust with a light but chewy interior—perfect for splitting and filling or as breakfast or dinner rolls with butter.

A ROUND ROLL

Weigh a piece of dough 1–2 oz. (30–50 g). Lightly flour the work surface and rub a little flour between the palms of your hands. If you are right-handed, hold the dough in your left hand, cupping your right hand around the dough and working the fingers underneath (1). Now circle your right hand around and around, keeping your fingers tucked underneath. The trick is to keep the cupped palm that the dough sits in relatively free of flour, and the curved fingers and palm that press and rotate the dough well floured. Gradually you will find that the ball of dough will tighten, and form a smooth skin on the upper surface (2). If you don't do this the roll will not hold its shape during baking. With practice, shaping a round roll should take just 5–10 seconds.

Lightly flour the cloth you will rest the dough on. Place the shaped roll with the smooth surface downward on the floured cloth. Shape the remaining pieces and place them face down on the cloth, leaving an inch or so between each to allow for the dough to rise and spread.

A LONG ROLL

Weigh a piece of dough 2–3 oz. (50–70 g). Flour your hands and, on a floured surface, pat the piece of dough out into a rough rectangle. Fold the two upper corners of the dough in toward the center, forming a triangular top with a flat base. Press these corners down firmly into the dough. Next fold the upper half down into the center of the dough (1). With the tips of your fingers, press the edge firmly down into the center.

Flip the dough around, so that the edge that was previously at the bottom is now at the top. Again fold the top two corners in toward the center and seal them down with your fingertips (2). Now fold the upper edge in toward the center and seal it firmly down with your fingers. Fold the dough in half, and seal the edges together with the palm of your hand, starting at one end and working your way carefully along to the other.

Turn the shaped dough over so that the seam you have just sealed is underneath. Cup your hands over the ends of the sausage shape, clawing your fingers around the dough. Press down lightly upon the dough and rock the dough gently back and forth, increasing the pressure on the edges of your palms so that the ends of the roll are narrowed. Twist them into points.

Lightly flour a cloth and put the shaped piece of dough on it with the smooth surface downward. Shape the remaining pieces and place them face down on the cloth, leaving an inch or so between each to allow for the dough to rise and spread.

Baking with wild yeasts

There are millions of microscopic yeast spores in the air. When the type called brewer's sugar fungus settles in a mixture of flour and water, slow fermentation results, during which carbon dioxide is given off and a distinct acid-sour flavor is imparted to the resulting bread. The first leavened breads were hit-or-miss affairs, raised accidentally by the random colonization and action of such airborne yeasts. It was the Egyptians who discovered 6,000 years ago that the froth produced on the top of beer during fermentation could leaven dough and cause it to rise, a breakthrough that meant bakers could control the process and achieve consistent results.

Since the mid-1800s, most breads have been baked using commercially produced cultured brewer's yeast, which generates gas more aggressively than wild yeasts. It raises dough quickly and consequently produces sweeter, less tangy, and lighter bread. Sourdough loaves, however, are still raised slowly using a starter dough colonized by wild yeasts.

Sourdough breads

Sourdough breads are leavened using the microscopic natural yeasts that are in the air all around us, and the breads get their name from the characteristic flavor they acquire during the lengthy fermentation and rising of the wheat-flour dough. These are robust, rustic breads that keep well, and are often baked as very large loaves—the French oval-shaped *miche* typically weighs 4½ pounds. Some cultures have always appreciated the unique taste, strong crust, and chewy texture of sourdoughs. The French *pain au levain*, the Italian *pagnotta*, and German rye breads are all examples of wild yeast baking at its best.

Bread has been leavened using wild yeasts for at least 6,000 years. How and why they made dough rise was not understood until 1857, when Louis Pasteur discovered that they generated carbon dioxide as a product of fermentation. When the type of wild yeast called brewer's sugar fungus, or brewer's yeast, settles in an appropriate environment, fermentation results, giving off carbon dioxide and delivering a distinct acid-sour flavor to the dough.

Brewer's yeast is the perfect leavening agent for high-gluten bread flours, because it generates gas slowly, over hours or even days. The gas is trapped as bubbles by the unique elastic and plastic qualities of the gluten, a combination of two proteins found in wheat grain. When moistened, they bind together to create thin, elastic strands. These form membranes that trap the gas, causing the dough to rise and producing leavened—as opposed to unleavened—bread. Putting risen dough in a hot oven makes the gas bubbles expand still further, and the dough cooks around them, leaving holes where the gas was and delivering light-textured loaves.

The first leavened breads were almost certainly raised accidentally by the random colonization and action of airborne yeasts, until the Egyptians discovered that the froth produced on the top of beer during fermentation when mixed into dough caused it to rise. Other societies made the same discovery entirely independently, though much later. The Celts, for example, were found by the Romans to use beer froth, or barm, in breadmaking. In England, in the twelfth century, dough was kneaded in a "souring trough," which was never washed, so that the fermented dough left on its surface activated the next batch of dough.

Beer froth continued to be widely used by bakers until the first half of the last century. Since then, most breads have been leavened using "active," commercially produced yeast, either in cultured or reconstituted dried forms. These raise dough quickly and consequently produce sweeter, less tangy, and less chewy loaves.

Sourdough loaves, however, are still raised using a starter batter or dough colonized by airborne yeasts. The starter batters are called "poolish" by bakers in the

U.S. and Britain. This comes from the Polish of Poland, a country renowned more for its rye baking than its sourdoughs, but which exported knowledge and technique with its bakers as they moved first through Europe and then across the Atlantic. It is the lengthy fermentation of the batter that develops the acids which give the bread its distinctive sour flavor.

Levain is the term used for a naturally fermented old dough starter, the name levain being taken from the French *lever*, meaning to lift. The secret in baking these delicious and remarkable breads is in providing the right environment for the airborne yeasts to take.

The amount of sourdough poolish or levain a particular recipe needs has been adjusted to give optimum results. Many professional bakers use a strict 2 percent of yeast to flour weight. At Baker & Spice we don't, because we feel such inflexibility only limits and restricts what can be produced. It

is, however, always the starting point when developing a recipe.

In the poolish recipes, precise ambient temperatures are given at different stages in the fermentation and rising process. This is not a science, however, and these are not absolutes, but the closer you can come to the recommended temperatures, the better the results will be. At all times keep the poolish out of drafts and try to avoid temperature fluctuation.

A poolish should not be cold when incorporated into a dough, so remove it from the refrigerator at least 2 hours before using. A levain, on the other hand, can be used straight from the fridge.

WILD YEAST STARTERS

Making wild yeast starters is neither difficult nor time-consuming, and has a satisfying quality about it. You are simply creating an environment that airborne yeasts like. The magic is in the consequences of the fermentation this produces. Some starters can be kept going almost indefinitely—it is said that sourdough starters have been handed down from one generation to the next.

Adding grapes or raisins to the batter will speed up the action of the airborne wild yeasts

San Francisco sourdough starter

Our San Francisco sourdough starter, which is a poolish, borrows the current American artisanal bakery practice of using yogurt, but this recipe was very much developed at Baker & Spice.

The poolish will raise dough as soon as the fermentation has begun; however, in the bakery we find that it takes a couple of weeks for a real flavor to develop. Sometimes bakers will give you pieces of wild yeast starter that have a developed flavor, and these can be beaten into the batter just before you add the fruit.

Vigorous and prolonged beating is important when making the starter because it incorporates the maximum amount of air. This will help to ensure that fermentation occurs quickly and aggressively. Later on, this vigorous activity is deliberately slowed as emphasis shifts away from the generation of carbon dioxide needed to raise the loaf and toward the development of flavor and texture in the finished bread.

1 TABLESPOON STONEGROUND RYE OR
   WHOLE-WHEAT FLOUR
2^1/$_2$ CUPS (300 G) WHITE BREAD FLOUR
1^1/$_4$ CUPS (300 G) PLAIN LOW-FAT YOGURT
SCANT 1 CUP (200 ML) APPLE CIDER
^{2}/$_3$ CUP (100 G) GRAPES OR RINSED AND
   DRAINED RAISINS

Put the flours, yogurt, and apple cider in the bowl of a heavy-duty electric mixer fitted with the whisk. On the slowest speed, beat for 10 minutes, when a slightly lumpy batter will have formed. Increase the speed and beat for a further 5 minutes or until the mixture is thick, elastic, and bubbly. Add the grapes or raisins, which will encourage the airborne yeasts to start working more quickly.

Pour and scrape the batter into a very clean 3-quart mixing bowl. Dust the top with a handful of white flour and cover the top of the bowl with plastic wrap. Place the bowl in a very warm place (82°F) and leave it for about 24 hours. This high temperature environment is necessary to kick-start the fermentation of the batter.

The next day the batter should have risen noticeably and may even have doubled in bulk. Beat for a minute with a hand whisk, then whisk in a refreshment mixture of:

^{2}/$_3$ CUP (150 G) PLAIN LOW-FAT YOGURT
^{2}/$_3$ CUP (150 ML) WHOLE MILK

Once completely incorporated, pour the mixture through a colander into a clean bowl and discard the fruit. Now add:

2^1/$_2$ CUPS (300 G) WHITE BREAD FLOUR

Stir the mixture together with a wooden spoon for a minute or two, breaking up any lumps of flour. Scrape down the sides of the bowl, then dust the top again with a handful of flour before covering the container with plastic wrap. Leave it in a warm place (about 70°F) for 24 hours. You now have an active starter, which can be stored in a plastic container covered with a lid in the refrigerator.

The starter can be used immediately, although it is better to wait, as it takes a couple of weeks for any special flavor characteristics to develop. Each day you need to refresh your starter: First remove 1–1¼ lb. (500–600 g) to bake with or to make sourdough pancakes (or just discard), then add the yogurt, milk, and flour mixture as before.

If you forget to refresh the starter, you will find that it separates and stops fermenting. It can be reactivated by beating in some more flour and yogurt plus a little apple cider. Alternatively, you can freeze the starter and then reactivate it once thawed and returned to room temperature.

Biga acida

The Italian version of poolish, this starter is based on "OO" flour, which you can buy from specialist mail-order suppliers.

JUICE OF 2 ORANGES
2 TEASPOONS WHOLE-WHEAT FLOUR
$^1/_2$ CUP (60 G) "00" FLOUR
1 TABLESPOON CLEAR HONEY
$^3/_4$ CUP (100 G) WHITE BREAD FLOUR
SCANT $^1/_2$ CUP (100 ML) BOTTLED SPRING
    WATER

Put all the ingredients in the bowl of a heavy-duty electric mixer fitted with the whisk. Whisk at the slowest speed for 1 minute to mix, then increase to medium fast and whisk for 8–10 minutes.

Transfer to a large plastic container, cover, and leave in a very warm place (82°F) for 24 hours. After this time the surface should be pocked with tiny holes as the yeasts start to activate. Leave for a further 24–48 hours to continue its development.

Pour the mixture into the bowl of the mixer fitted with the paddle and add the refreshment ingredients:

SCANT $^1/_2$ CUP (100 ML) BOTTLED SPRING
    WATER
1$^1/_4$ CUPS (150 G) "00" FLOUR

Mix at a slow speed for 3–4 minutes, then return to the plastic container and put the lid back on. Leave at room temperature for 4–6 hours, then refrigerate overnight.

The poolish is now ready to use.

Rye starter

Germany, like Poland, has a strong tradition of dark rye breads, heavy and strong in flavor. This starter, which is a poolish, needs quite a lot of help to get it going, and it is essential to use organic ingredients—chemicals will prevent yeast colonization.

After a time in the refrigerator the poolish may stop working. If it fails to double in size over 24 hours in the fridge, leave it in a warm place for 6–8 hours until it reactivates. It will gain strength from being refreshed every day.

Low-fat yogurt is specified because less fat delivers greater activity in the dough.

1 CUP (125 G) WHITE BREAD FLOUR

1¹/₄ CUPS (125 G) STONEGROUND RYE FLOUR
+ EXTRA FOR SPRINKLING

²/₃ CUP (150 ML) APPLE CIDER

²/₃ CUP (150 G) PLAIN LOW-FAT YOGURT

¹/₂ CUP (50 G) CURRANTS, WELL RINSED AND
DRAINED

In the bowl of a heavy-duty electric mixer fitted with the paddle, combine the flours, apple cider, and yogurt. Whisk at a medium speed for 10–12 minutes. Stir in the currants, then transfer the mixture to a plastic container. Sprinkle the surface with a handful of rye flour to make a layer about ¼ inch deep. Put a lid on the container so the contents are covered but not sealed airtight, then leave in a very warm place (82°F) for 24 hours.

The next day, beat the mixture in the container for 3–4 minutes, by hand or using a spatula or fork. Sprinkle a little more rye flour on top, replace the lid, and leave for another 24 hours.

Sprinkle 1–2 tablespoons rye flour on top, and put the lid back on as before. Once again, leave for 24 hours.

By the third day the mixture should be bubbly and have almost doubled in volume. Remove half of the mixture—this can be used in a sourdough pancake batter or be just thrown away. Put the remaining mixture through a colander into a bowl, discarding the currants. It is now ready for the refreshment:

²/₃ CUP (150 ML) APPLE CIDER

²/₃ CUP (150 G) PLAIN LOW-FAT YOGURT

1 CUP (125 G) WHITE BREAD FLOUR

1¹/₄ CUPS (125 G) STONEGROUND RYE FLOUR

Whisk together the apple cider and yogurt, and add to the bowl along with the flours. Stir together, then return the mixture to the plastic container. Cover with the lid and put into the refrigerator.

Each day for the next 5 days, remove half of the poolish and discard it, whisk in the same refreshment of apple cider, yogurt, and flour, then return to the fridge to ferment. By the sixth day, the poolish is ready for inclusion in dough to be baked.

Jason's basic French levain

This is an excellent workhorse starter, reliable and easy to maintain. Levain fermentation is slower than that which occurs with active yeast, although using organic ingredients will help the yeasts to get working more quickly. Yeasts respond well to a splash of freshly squeezed orange juice because of the vitamin C it contains. While the accelerating effect is initially desirable, the amount of juice used in successive refreshments should be progressively reduced.

You can either make this by hand or in a heavy-duty electric mixer. Using a mixer will incorporate the maximum amount of air, and with it airborne yeasts.

3/4 CUP (100 G) WHITE BREAD FLOUR
1/3 CUP (40 G) WHOLE-WHEAT FLOUR
3 TABLESPOONS BOTTLED SPRING WATER
1 TABLESPOON CLEAR HONEY
3 TABLESPOONS FRESHLY SQUEEZED ORANGE
   JUICE

If making by hand, mound the flours on a work surface. Make a depression in the mound and carefully pour in the water, honey, and orange juice. Gently combine the ingredients with your fingers. As you work, the flour and water will turn into a paste, then into a ball of dough. Now knead the dough, not too aggressively, for 7–8 minutes. When you have finished kneading, the dough will be resilient and will spring back when touched. If using a heavy-duty electric mixer, put all the ingredients in the bowl and knead with the dough hook for 8 minutes at medium speed.

The dough is now a fledgling levain. Put it in a small, dry bowl and cover with plastic wrap. Leave in a warm place for 2–3 days.

When the levain is ready, there will be evident aeration and a distinctly sweet smell of fermentation, and it will have increased in size by about half (1). It is now ready for the first refreshment, which will give the yeast spores fresh material to work with.

4 TEASPOONS FRESHLY SQUEEZED ORANGE
   JUICE
4 TEASPOONS BOTTLED SPRING WATER
7 TABLESPOONS (50 G) WHITE BREAD FLOUR
3 TABLESPOONS (20 G) WHOLE-WHEAT FLOUR

Dilute the orange juice with the spring water, then mix with the flours on the work surface to make a loose dough. Knead this together with the active levain until the two are thoroughly integrated. Put in a clean, dry container and cover with plastic wrap. Leave in a warm place for 15–20 hours or until the levain has risen appreciably and is full of bubbles when you cut into it (2).

Repeat the refreshment procedure, using the same amounts, then cover the bowl with fresh plastic wrap and leave to ferment at the same temperature for 8–12 hours. By this time the levain will have doubled in size and have a slightly sour smell and flavor. It is now ready to use for baking. If not using immediately, store in the refrigerator.

WILD YEAST BREADS

Wild yeast breads have stronger flavors than those leavened with commercial yeast. With their more robust crust and chewy, well-aerated crumb, these are loaves with real character and individuality.

Pagnotta

A classic well-flavored loaf, this is baked with minor regional variations throughout Italy—the Italian version of a French pain de campagne. An experienced baker used to working with wetter doughs could increase the amount of water to ²/₃ cup (150 ml). The wetter the dough, the greater the aeration.

MAKES 2 LOAVES

1 LB. 2 OZ. (500 G) BIGA ACIDA (PAGE 35), AT WARM ROOM TEMPERATURE
2 CUPS (250 G) WHITE BREAD FLOUR + EXTRA FOR DUSTING
2 CUPS (250 G) "00" FLOUR
¹/₂ CUP (125 ML) WARM BOTTLED SPRING WATER (ABOUT 68°F)
1 TABLESPOON CLEAR HONEY
1 TABLESPOON SALT
OLIVE OIL FOR THE BOWL
POLENTA FOR THE PEEL

In the bowl of a heavy-duty electric mixer fitted with the paddle, combine the biga and flours. Beating at slow speed, slowly add the water and beat together. Change to the dough hook. Increase the speed of the mixer to medium and beat for 8 minutes, when the biga will have broken down and the dough will be smooth and elastic. Add the honey and salt, and beat for another minute.

Rub the inside of a large mixing bowl with olive oil. Empty the dough into the bowl and turn it over several times to film the surface with oil. Cover the bowl with plastic wrap and place in a warm part of the kitchen to rise. Leave undisturbed for 1 hour.

Transfer the dough to a lightly floured work surface. It may not have risen much by now, but the fermentation will accelerate over the next 3 hours. Dust the top of the dough and your hands with flour, then tap the dough out firmly with the palm and heel of your hand until it forms a rough rectangle. Fold in half, then into three in the other direction, until the dough is folded like a blanket. Return to the bowl, cover with plastic wrap, and let rise in a warm place for another hour.

Repeat the folding and deflating process each hour for the next 3 hours, re-covering the top each time with plastic wrap.

Tip the dough out onto a floured work surface and lightly knead into a ball. Cut the dough in half. Shape each piece into a bâton (page 27). Flour two dough-rising baskets and lay the loaves in them. Cover the baskets with a damp cloth and let rise in a warm place for 3–4 hours.

Preheat the oven to 500°F, with a baking stone or heavy baking sheet on the central rack.

Test to see if the dough is ready for baking by pressing a finger lightly against the surface. The dough should slowly spring back to its original shape. Dust a rimless metal cookie sheet with polenta: this will act as the peel.

Briefly spray the baking stone or sheet and the sides and bottom of the oven with water, then quickly close the oven door. Upturn one basket so the loaf falls centrally onto the peel. Lift up the loaf and stretch it about 2 inches lengthwise. Set it back down on the peel. Hold the loaf on its peel next to the oven, open the door, and swiftly slide the loaf onto one side of the hot stone, closing the door immediately. After 2 minutes, open the oven door and spray the bread and the sides of the oven with water, again quickly shutting the door to keep heat loss to a minimum. Repeat with the other loaf. Leave to bake for 10 minutes. Turn down the oven temperature to 350°F and bake for a further 25 minutes or until the loaves feel firm when pressed and sound hollow when tapped on the base.

Remove the bread from the oven and let cool to room temperature on a wire rack before slicing for serving.

San Francisco sourdough

San Francisco has been celebrated for its sourdough breads ever since the Gold Rush, when prospectors took pieces of starter dough from the city with them to the mountains of Northern California, to bake with. This explains the name—which universally describes a loaf made primarily from white flour and raised with wild yeasts—but embraces a number of different techniques.

MAKES 2 LARGE LOAVES

SPONGE

$3^1/4$ CUPS (400 G) WHITE BREAD FLOUR

2 CUPS (500 ML) WARM BOTTLED SPRING WATER (ABOUT 68°F)

10 OZ. (300 G) SAN FRANCISCO SOURDOUGH STARTER (PAGE 34), AT WARM ROOM TEMPERATURE

DOUGH

$3^1/4$ CUPS (400 G) WHITE BREAD FLOUR + EXTRA FOR DUSTING

1 TABLESPOON SALT

SEMOLINA FOR THE PEEL

Put the sponge ingredients in a bowl and mix together with a whisk. Cover with a damp cloth and leave in a warm place for 4–5 hours, when the sponge should be bubbling and obviously working.

Pour the sponge into the bowl of a heavy-duty electric mixer and add half the quantity of flour. Using the paddle attachment, mix together on a low speed for 2 minutes or until the mixture begins to cohere. Increase the speed to medium and beat for 8 minutes. Add the rest of the flour and the salt. Change to the dough hook and beat the dough for 8 minutes on low speed. Increase the speed to medium and beat for a further 2 minutes. You should have an elastic dough that will form a membrane when stretched between the fingers.

Tip the dough out of the bowl onto a 12 x 18-inch tray. Lightly dust the top of the dough with flour, cover with a damp cloth, and leave in a warm place for 1 hour. During this first fermentation, sugars are broken down and converted to carbon dioxide and alcohol. The gas provides the lift, but it is the alcohol that bonds with the gluten as organic acids, causing it to contract. This makes the dough more plastic and elastic, both resilient and stretchy.

Dust the work surface lightly with flour, and tip the dough off the tray onto it. Rub a little flour onto your hands, then pat the dough out to flatten it into a rectangle and gently deflate it. Fold it in half, then into three in the opposite direction, like a blanket. Flip this parcel over, put it back on the floured tray, and cover with a damp cloth. Let rise in a warm place for another hour.

Repeat the folding and deflating process every hour for 2 more hours, then tip the dough out onto the floured surface. Divide the dough into two pieces and shape each into a bâton (page 27). Line two dough-rising baskets with a dish towel and dust generously with flour. Place the loaves in the baskets with the smooth upper surface down. Dust the loaves with more flour, then cover each with another dish towel. Let rise in a warm place for 3–4 hours, when they will have almost doubled in bulk.

Preheat the oven to 500°F with a baking stone or heavy baking sheet on the middle shelf. The plan is to bake both loaves at the same time, and to do this you need to slide the first loaf to sit on the back half of the baking stone. You can't do everything at once, so shut the oven door in between each action to keep heat loss to a minimum.

Dust two rimless metal cookie sheets with semolina: these will act as peels. Tip one loaf from its basket onto a peel. Repeat with the second loaf onto the other peel. Open the oven door and slide the first loaf onto the back of the baking stone. Close the oven door while you get the second loaf, then slide this onto the front of the stone. Spray everything liberally with water, then quickly shut the oven door and bake for 10 minutes. Lower the

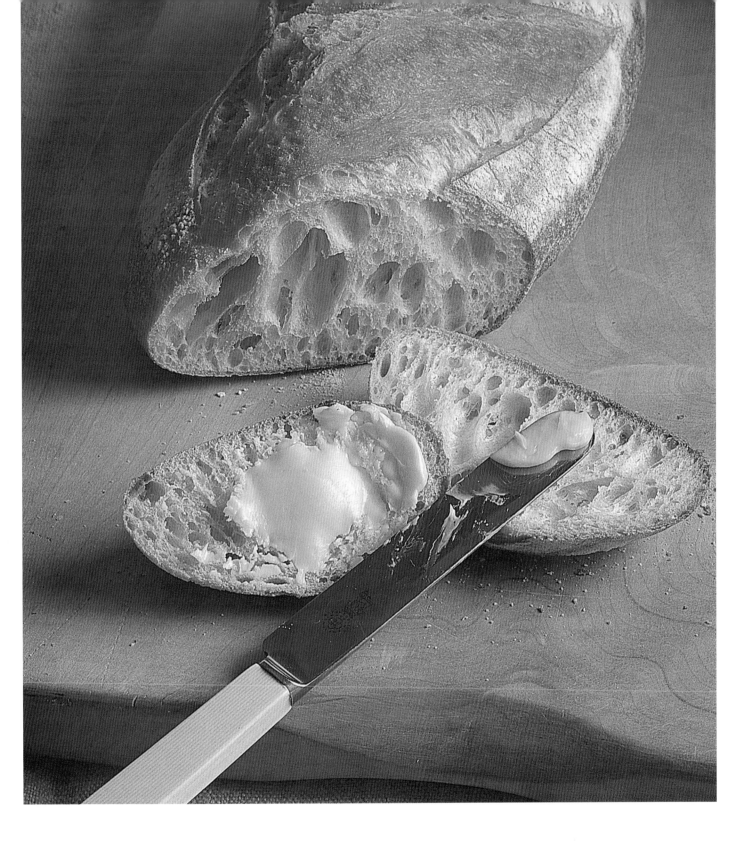

oven temperature to 350°F and bake for a further 40 minutes. Don't worry if the crust becomes very dark—the color of the loaves will lighten a little after they are removed from the oven. The long bake helps the bread to keep better, preserving the texture of the crust. When done, the loaves will sound hollow when tapped on the base.

Transfer to a wire rack and let cool to room temperature before slicing.

Pain au levain

A classic, thick-crusted pain au levain is a long-lasting rustic bread. It has a terrific depth of flavor and a moist yet firm and springy crumb, with a texture more compact than some country-style breads.

MAKES 2 LOAVES

3/4 CUP (100 G) WHOLE-WHEAT BREAD FLOUR
3 CUPS (400 G) WHITE BREAD FLOUR + EXTRA FOR DUSTING
1/4 CUP (25 G) WHEAT GERM
1 CUP (250 ML) WARM BOTTLED SPRING WATER (ABOUT 68°F)
1/4 CUP (60 ML) FRESHLY SQUEEZED ORANGE JUICE
1 LB. 2 OZ. (500 G) JASON'S BASIC FRENCH LEVAIN (PAGE 37)
1 TABLESPOON SALT
SUNFLOWER OIL FOR THE BOWL
SEMOLINA FOR THE PEEL

In the bowl of a heavy-duty electric mixer fitted with the paddle, combine the whole-wheat and white flours, wheat germ, water, and orange juice. Beat at a low speed for 6 minutes. Now add the levain and continue beating for 4 minutes. Add the salt, increase the speed to medium, and beat for another 4–5 minutes. The dough should be very elastic and quite firm to the touch.

Lightly brush a 3-quart mixing bowl with sunflower oil and transfer the dough to it, covering the top with plastic wrap. Let rise in a warm place for 1 hour.

Place the dough on a lightly floured surface and knead for 8–10 minutes until the mass feels soft and elastic. Clean the bowl and lightly brush with sunflower oil. Return the dough to the bowl, cover tightly with plastic wrap, and put in a warm place to rise for 2 hours.

Turn out the dough onto a lightly floured surface. With the heel of your hand, pin out the dough into a rectangle to gently deflate it. Fold in half, then into three in the opposite direction. Each time you fold, press down to remove air. Dust the bowl with flour and return the dough to it. Cover and let rise in a warm place for 1 hour.

Repeat the folding and deflating process, then let rise for a final hour.

Divide the dough into two pieces, each weighing about 1½ lb. (just over 700 g). Lay a clean dish towel on a small tray. Liberally dredge the towel with flour. Shape each piece of dough into a tight, round loaf (page 26) and place "gathered" side up on the towel. Pull the towel up between the loaves to form little folds of cloth around them. These will steady and protect the loaves as they expand. Dust the exposed tops of the loaves with flour and cover with another dish towel. Set in a warm place to rise until doubled in size, which will take 5–6 hours.

Preheat the oven to 500°F, with a baking stone or heavy baking sheet on the middle shelf.

When the oven is at the correct temperature, uncover the dough. Sprinkle a little semolina on a rimless metal cookie sheet: this will act as your peel. Take one loaf and gently place it, gathered side down, on the peel. With a razor blade, cut 4 shallow slashes in a square shape around the loaf, about one-fourth of the way down from the top.

Open the oven door and quickly spray the hot baking stone and the sides and bottom of the oven with water, shutting the door immediately. Carry the loaf on its peel to the oven and slide it onto one end of the hot baking stone, immediately shutting the oven door. Repeat with the second loaf. After both loaves have been in the oven for 5 minutes, reduce the oven temperature to 400°F and bake for a further 55–60 minutes. When the loaves have finished baking they will be dark brown, will feel firm when pressed, and sound hollow when tapped on the base.

Transfer to a wire rack to cool to room temperature before slicing.

(Opposite) Pain au levain, top, Apple sourdough

Apple sourdough

You do not need a lot of rye flour to make an impact—even the small amount used here gives the bread character without making it too heavy or dominating the flavor. The crumb is the perfect foil for the fruit, its sweetness balancing the acidity of the sourdough and making this a great bread to eat with cheese. This is a heavy dough, so you need an active poolish at least 4 weeks old. Extra lift can be given by the inclusion of some quick-rising active dry yeast.

Granny Smith apples can be used instead of Bramley's if the latter are not available.

MAKES 2 LOAVES

8 OZ. (250 G) RYE STARTER
(PAGE 36), AT WARM ROOM
TEMPERATURE
$1/2$ PACKAGE QUICK-RISING ACTIVE
DRY YEAST (OPTIONAL)
SCANT 1 CUP (200 ML) WARM
BOTTLED SPRING WATER
(ABOUT 68°F)
3 CUPS (375 G) WHITE BREAD
FLOUR + EXTRA FOR DUSTING
1 CUP (125 G) WHOLE-WHEAT
BREAD FLOUR
$1/2$ CUP (50 G) RYE FLOUR
2 TABLESPOONS APPLE CIDER
2 TEASPOONS SALT
7 OZ. (200 G) BRAMLEY'S OR
GRANNY SMITH APPLES
(PEELED WEIGHT)
SUNFLOWER OIL FOR THE BOWL
SEMOLINA FOR THE PEEL

Whisk the starter and yeast into the warm water with half of the white flour. Cover and leave in a warm place for 1 hour or until the mixture bubbles.

Place the remaining white flour in a 4-quart bowl with the whole-wheat and rye flours. Add the starter mixture, the apple cider, and the salt. Stir with your hands until the mixture forms a rough ball of dough in the center of the bowl.

Turn the dough out onto a lightly floured surface and knead for 8–10 minutes or until it feels soft and elastic. Clean the bowl and lightly brush with sunflower oil. Put the dough back in the bowl, tightly cover with plastic wrap, and leave in a warm place for 1 hour.

Peel, quarter, and core the apples, then cut each quarter into 3 or 4 slices.

Turn out the dough onto the lightly floured surface. With the heel of your hand, pin out the dough into a rectangle to gently deflate it. Press the apple pieces into the dough, leaving about $3/4$ inch between them. Fold one long side in by a third, then take the opposite side and fold that over the first. Repeat the folding action with the ends. Dust the bowl with flour and return the dough to it. Cover the top with plastic wrap and let rise in a warm place for 1 hour. Repeat the pinning and folding process, and let rise for another hour.

Turn the dough out onto the floured surface. Divide the dough into two pieces and shape each into a bâton (page 27). Lay a clean dish towel on a tray and liberally dredge it with flour. Place the loaves seam-side up on the towel. Pull the towel up between the loaves to form little folds between them. These will support and separate the loaves as they expand. Dust the tops of the loaves with flour, cover with another dish towel, and let rise in a warm place until doubled in size, which will take $2^{1}/2$–3 hours.

Put a baking stone or large baking sheet on the central rack of the oven and preheat it to 500°F. When the oven has come up to temperature, sprinkle a little semolina on a rimless metal cookie sheet: this will act as your peel. Gently tip one loaf top-side down onto the peel. With a razor blade, cut three shallow slashes at an angle at regular intervals along the top.

Working quickly, spray water on the baking stone or sheet and on the sides and bottom of the oven, then shut the door. Fetch the first loaf and slide it onto the baking stone. Repeat with the second loaf. After both loaves have been in the oven for 5 minutes, spray them with water and reduce the oven temperature to 400°F. Bake for a further 45–55 minutes. The loaves have finished baking when they have taken on a strong color, feel firm when pressed, and sound hollow when tapped on the base.

Transfer to a wire rack to cool to room temperature before slicing.

On bread dough

"Dough is not something that you just leave alone. It has to be nurtured. And yet there is alchemy in baking, acts of creation. You impose your will only up to a certain point because a dough can appear to have a life of its own—things will happen spontaneously.

"I use the analogy of gardening to baking— you know where you want to get to, but the plants do things that are beyond your control. There is a natural balance in bread you should never lose sight of." DAN LEPARD, BAKER

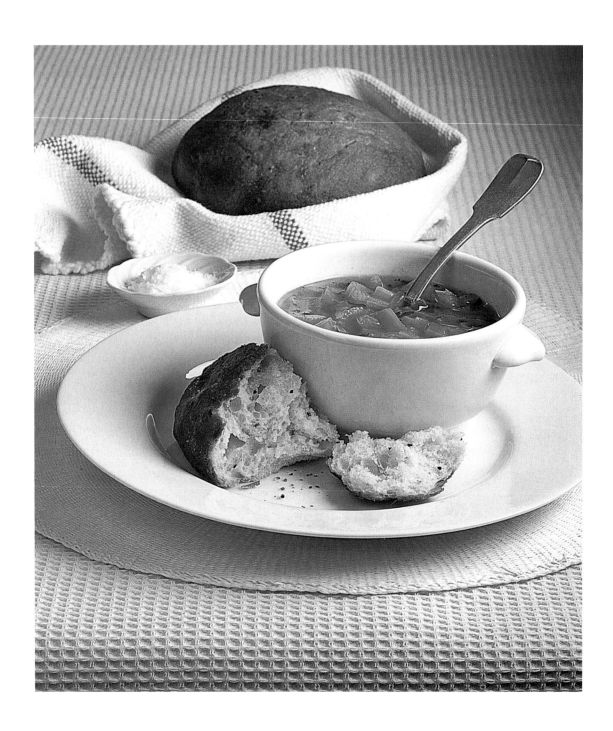

Potato and rosemary bread

This is adapted from a recipe given to Gail Stephens by Erez Komarovsky, whose bakery in Tel Aviv produces extraordinary sourdough breads. The Baker & Spice potato and rosemary bread retains the freshness and big flavors of the original, but it is identifiably ours.

MAKES 1 LOAF

8 OZ. (250 G) BIGA ACIDA (PAGE 35), AT WARM ROOM TEMPERATURE
SCANT $^1/_2$ CUP (100 ML) BOTTLED SPRING WATER
2 CUPS (250 G) WHITE BREAD FLOUR + EXTRA FOR DUSTING
$^2/_3$ CUP (100 G) BAKED POTATO FLESH CUT IN PIECES
2 TABLESPOONS EXTRA VIRGIN OLIVE OIL + EXTRA FOR BRUSHING
1 TABLESPOON CHOPPED FRESH ROSEMARY
1 TABLESPOON BLACK ONION SEEDS (NIGELLA)
1 TABLESPOON SALT
SEMOLINA FOR DUSTING

Put all the ingredients except the salt into the bowl of a heavy-duty electric mixer fitted with the dough hook. Work on the slowest speed for 4 minutes, then increase to medium and work for a further 5 minutes, when the dough will be elastic and satin-smooth. Add the salt and mix for a final 2 minutes.

Brush the inside of a 3-quart bowl with olive oil. Scrape the dough out of the mixer and into the bowl. Lightly oil your hands and rub the top of the dough. Pull the sides of the dough down and tuck them under the base, like tucking in the sheets on a bed. Repeat the movement five or six times, rotating the bowl as you do so. Cover the top of the bowl with plastic wrap and let rise in a warm place for 1 hour.

Repeat the tucking process twice, rising for an hour each time.

Tip the dough onto the lightly floured surface and shape into a round loaf (page 26). Line a dough-rising basket with a dish towel and dust generously with semolina. Place the loaf in the basket with the smooth upper surface facing down. Dust the loaf with more semolina, then cover with another dish towel. Set in a warm place to rise until doubled in size, which will take about 4 hours.

Put a baking stone or large heavy baking sheet on a central rack in the oven, and preheat the oven to 500°F.

Scatter semolina on a rimless metal cookie sheet: this will act as a peel. Using the dish towel to help, roll the loaf onto your hand, then lay it, top-side down, on the peel.

Spray the hot baking stone or sheet and sides and bottom of the oven with water, then quickly shut the door. Leave for a minute for steam to be generated, then slide the dough off the peel onto the stone and shut the door immediately. After 5 minutes reduce the oven temperature to 400°F. Bake for a further 45–55 minutes. The bread is done when it has developed a good color and the crust feels firm. It should sound hollow when tapped on the base.

Transfer to a wire rack and brush the top lightly with olive oil. This will give the crust an appealing shine and accentuate the color. Let cool to room temperature before slicing.

Baking with commercial leavening

Commercial leavening describes the use of cultured baker's yeast, the living cells of the yeast strain *Saccharomyces cerevisiae*. Baker's yeast is sold in two forms: moist, compressed cakes of fresh yeast, which will keep for several weeks in a refrigerator, and active dry yeast in which the yeast cells are dormant due to lack of moisture. Although it is possible to buy compressed fresh yeast, rapid fermentation and consistent results are best achieved in a domestic kitchen using active dry yeast granules. The instant or quick-rising version is the simplest to use, as it can be mixed in with all the other dry ingredients. For many bread doughs, however, we prefer to make a sponge of the yeast, a little flour, and some liquid, as this speeds the initial fermentation and results in a better loaf.

BREADS

Good bread is more than an accompaniment or adjunct to other foods, for it helps to shape our enjoyment and perception of the dish we are eating it with. Soup, charcuterie, and cheese are all reduced in its absence. A sandwich, no matter how fine the filling, can only ever be as good as the slices of bread that define it.

Organic whole-wheat bread

A dense-textured loaf, this slices well for sandwiches or toast. It can be baked in a loaf pan to give a traditional shape or baked as a free-form oval. All the ingredients in the Baker & Spice loaf are organic, although you can, of course, use non-organic materials.

MAKES 2 LARGE LOAVES

1 PACKAGE QUICK-RISING ACTIVE
DRY YEAST
$2^1/_2$ CUPS (600 ML) WARM
BOTTLED SPRING WATER
(ABOUT 68°F)
$4^1/_3$ CUPS (550 G) WHITE BREAD
FLOUR + EXTRA FOR DUSTING
4 CUPS (500 G) WHOLE-WHEAT
BREAD FLOUR
$^2/_3$ CUP (20 G) BRAN FLAKES
5 TEASPOONS SALT
SCANT $^1/_2$ CUP (100 ML) FRESHLY
SQUEEZED ORANGE JUICE
ROLLED OATS FOR COATING
SUNFLOWER OIL FOR THE BOWL

Whisk the yeast into the warm water followed by $2^1/_2$ cups (300 g) of the white flour. Leave in a warm place for 20–30 minutes or until the mixture froths.

Put all the dry ingredients, including the remaining white flour, in a 4-quart bowl. Add the yeast batter and the orange juice. Stir with your hands, mixing to form a rough ball of dough. Transfer it to a lightly floured work surface and knead for 8–10 minutes or until the mass feels soft and elastic. It is hard work, but good exercise.

Clean the bowl and lightly brush with oil. Put the dough in the bowl, tightly cover the top with plastic wrap, and leave in a warm place for 1–$1^1/_2$ hours. The dough should have risen, although it won't quite double in bulk. If you cut into a corner of the dough, you should see bubbles forming inside.

Lightly oil two 2-pound loaf pans. Wet a dish towel and lay it out on the work surface. Lay another dish towel next to this and sprinkle it with a layer of oats.

Turn the dough onto a lightly floured surface. Divide the dough into two pieces and shape each into a bâton (page 27). Gently roll each shaped loaf on the dampened towel to moisten it, then roll in the oats to coat all over. Drop a loaf into each prepared pan, then cover with a clean dish towel. Let rise in a warm place until doubled in size, which will take 1–$1^1/_2$ hours.

Preheat the oven to maximum—at least 500°F, the hotter the better.

Check the dough by poking it with a finger and watching how slowly the mark disappears. You are looking for it to come back slowly to its previous shape, but it must have some spring left in it, not an exhausted, last-gasp return. The loaves will continue to expand for the first 10–15 minutes in the oven, and will need reserves of undeveloped gluten to do this.

Spray the inside of the oven generously with water, then quickly shut the door. Carry the loaves to the oven and slide them in quickly, immediately shutting the door. After 5 minutes, reduce the oven temperature to 400°F and bake for a further 45–55 minutes or until the loaves are well colored, have a firm crust, and sound hollow when you tip them out of the pan and tap the base. Transfer to a wire rack to cool to room temperature before slicing.

Pain blanc

The special texture of a baguette comes from slow-milled French flour T550, which is also referred to simply as baguette flour. Bakers may be able to get it for you, though you may have to buy it in sacks, or you can look for it in a specialist food store or mail-order supplier. A unique characteristic of the flour is its comparatively low rate of absorption of water.

Baguettes are made using a two-stage leavening: the sponge is made with half the amount of active dry yeast required, with the second half added later during kneading. The crisp crust can best be consistently achieved using T550 flour. However, while it is not authentic, we have found that all-purpose flour will deliver a very acceptable baguette in a domestic oven. The trick is to keep the dough temperature quite cold. This is best achieved by mixing with cold water to compensate for the heat generated by the rapid action of an electric mixer.

Other factors critical to producing the brittle crust and light, open texture that characterize a good baguette are the initial dough temperature and the maximum heat your oven can achieve for the first 20 minutes of baking. Steam is also important, and this can be delivered by the liberal use of a spray bottle of water.

Achieving the right shape does not require the use of metal molds—their use in large-scale commercial production is frowned upon by every artisanal baker. You can always tell a loaf risen in a mold by the tell-tale pattern of raised dots on its base. By simply rucking a cloth between pieces of dough you can achieve an authentic shape.

MAKES 4 BAGUETTES

SPONGE
$1/2$ PACKAGE QUICK-RISING
ACTIVE DRY YEAST
$3/4$ CUP (175 ML) WARM
BOTTLED SPRING WATER
(ABOUT 68°F)
$1^1/4$ CUPS (175 G) ALL-PURPOSE
FLOUR

DOUGH
$3/4$ CUP (175 ML) COLD
BOTTLED SPRING WATER
(ABOUT 50°F)
$1/2$ PACKAGE QUICK-RISING
ACTIVE DRY YEAST
$2^1/2$ CUPS (375 G) ALL-PURPOSE
FLOUR + EXTRA FOR DUSTING
$2^1/2$ TEASPOONS SALT
SUNFLOWER OIL FOR THE BOWL
SEMOLINA FOR THE PEEL

Make the sponge: in a 2-quart bowl, whisk together the yeast and warm water until the yeast has dissolved. Stir in the flour. Cover the bowl with plastic wrap and leave in a warm place for 2 hours or until the sponge has risen by at least one-third and is clearly active, with lots of bubbles.

Pour the sponge into the bowl of a heavy-duty electric mixer fitted with the whisk. Add the cold water and the second quantity of yeast, and whisk at slow speed for a minute or until the sponge is fully combined with the water. Change the whisk for the dough hook. Add the flour for the dough and work at a low speed until a rough ball of dough forms around the hook, about 2–3 minutes. Then add the salt, turn the machine up to medium, and knead for 9–10 minutes or until the dough is smooth and quite elastic. Transfer the dough to a lightly oiled bowl and cover the top with plastic wrap. Leave in a warm place for 30–40 minutes, just time for the dough to relax.

Tip the dough from the bowl onto a floured surface, ideally a large wooden chopping board. Divide the dough into four, each piece weighing roughly 6 oz. (170 g). Shape each lightly into an oval and place smooth-side down on a floured dinner plate. Cover with a damp cloth and set aside in a cool place to rest for 15 minutes.

Take a large dish towel or linen cloth and sprinkle flour on the surface. Lightly shake off any excess flour, then lay the cloth, flour-side up, on a large tray. Pull up the cloth every 2 inches to create folds about 2 inches high.

Take one piece of dough and place it smooth-side down on the lightly floured work surface. Shape it into a baguette (page 27). Carefully lift the loaf onto the floured cloth, setting it seam upward in the depression of one of the folds. Repeat the shaping with the remaining pieces of dough. (Alternatively, shape into rolls, page 29.) When the loaves are all on the floured cloth, cover them with a slightly damp cloth to protect them from the dry air. Let rise in a cool, draft-free place for about 2 hours or until they are doubled in bulk.

Put a large baking stone or heavy baking sheet on a centrally positioned rack in the oven, and preheat the oven to maximum—at least 500°F.

Scatter some semolina on a rimless metal cookie sheet, which will act as your peel. Using the cloth to help you, roll the first loaf top-side down onto the peel. With a razor blade, cut five to seven shallow slashes at an angle at regular intervals along the top.

Open the oven door and spray the baking stone or sheet and interior of the oven with water, then quickly close the door. Carry the first loaf to the oven and slide it onto the far side of the baking stone, closing the door quickly again. Repeat with the other loaves, shutting the door in between each loading. When the baguettes have been in the oven for 3–4 minutes, spray them with water. After they have baked for 10 minutes, reduce the oven temperature to 400°F. Bake for a further 15–20 minutes or until the baguettes have taken on a strong, golden color, their crust feels firm, and the loaves sound hollow when tapped on the base. (Rolls will take 30–35 minutes total baking time.)

Transfer to a wire rack to cool.

French wheaten rye

This bread uses both a poolish and a small amount of dry yeast to get maximum lift into the intrinsically heavy dough. It has a distinct rye taste, which is given further flavor and acidity by the wild yeast starter. In France, this is the kind of bread that would be called pain de campagne—rustic, chewy, and mellow.

MAKES 1 LOAF

$^{1}/_{2}$ PACKAGE QUICK-RISING ACTIVE DRY YEAST

$^{2}/_{3}$ CUP (150 ML) WARM BOTTLED SPRING WATER (ABOUT 68°F)

$1^{1}/_{2}$ CUPS (200 G) WHITE BREAD FLOUR + EXTRA FOR DUSTING

$^{1}/_{2}$ CUP (50 G) RYE FLOUR + EXTRA FOR THE CLOTH

$1^{1}/_{2}$ TEASPOONS SALT

10 OZ. (280 G) RYE STARTER (PAGE 36), AT WARM ROOM TEMPERATURE

SUNFLOWER OIL FOR THE BOWL

SEMOLINA FOR THE PEEL

Make the sponge: in a large bowl whisk together the yeast and warm water until the yeast has dissolved. Stir in 1¼ cups (150 g) of the white flour. Cover the bowl with plastic wrap and leave in a warm place for 2 hours or until the sponge has risen by at least one-third and is clearly active, with lots of bubbles.

Put all the remaining ingredients into the bowl of a heavy-duty electric mixer fitted with the dough hook, and add the sponge. Turn on at medium speed. Mix for about 5 minutes, when the dough will have formed a rough ball. Turn the speed up to maximum and mix for a further 2 minutes. Transfer the resulting sticky dough to a lightly oiled bowl. Cover the top with plastic wrap and let rise in a warm place for 2 hours.

Take a large linen cloth or dish towel—about 16 x 20 inches—and lay it on a tray. Rub some rye flour into it and reserve.

Tip the dough out onto a lightly floured work surface and tap it out with your hands to form a rough rectangle about 7 x 10 inches. Shape into a bâton (page 27). Put the dough, seam-side down, on the floured cloth. Cover with another cloth and let rise in a warm place for 3½–4 hours.

Preheat the oven to maximum—at least 500°F—with a baking stone or heavy metal baking sheet on a centrally positioned rack. Sprinkle semolina on a rimless cookie sheet to use as a peel.

Roll the loaf onto your hand, using the cloth to help, so the base is on your palm, then upend it onto one side of the peel. Working quickly, open the oven door and slide the loaf onto the stone, then immediately shut the door while you get the spray bottle. Spray the sides and bottom of the oven liberally with water, taking no more than 5 seconds, to keep heat loss to a minimum. Shut the door immediately and bake for 10 minutes.

Lower the oven temperature to 350°F and continue baking for 40–45 minutes or until the bread is dark brown and sounds hollow when you tap the base. Transfer the loaf to a wire rack to cool to room temperature before slicing.

Make "fresh" crumbs from slices of day-old bread. Remove the crust, then leave uncovered at room temperature for 24 hours to dry sufficiently to blitz in a food processor. The resulting crumbs will still have a high moisture content, so will go moldy if put into a jar. To dry them for storage, spread them on a baking sheet in a low oven for 1–2 hours, after which they will keep in an airtight container for several weeks.

Alternatively, put slices of bread, crusts on, on a baking sheet and bake them at 325°F until browned, then blitz to a crumb. This produces the finest crumbs—the best for coating fish cakes or any food that is to be breaded for shallow or deep-frying.

French wheaten rye, on left, and English granary and sunflower seed bread

English granary and sunflower seed bread

A loaf of pleasing textural contrasts and strong flavors, this is good to slice for sandwiches. The inclusion of rye flour and malt makes for a darker color and closer texture. If you cannot get English granary flour, which is a mix of whole-wheat flour, malt, and barley, you can substitute whole-wheat flour plus ½ cup (50 g) malted wheat flakes, or use graham flour.

MAKES 1 LOAF

$^1/_2$ PACKAGE QUICK-RISING
ACTIVE DRY YEAST
$1^1/_4$ CUPS (300 ML) WARM
BOTTLED SPRING
WATER (ABOUT 68°F)
$^3/_4$ CUP (100 G) WHITE BREAD
FLOUR + EXTRA
FOR DUSTING
$2^1/_2$ CUPS (300 G) GRANARY
FLOUR
$^1/_2$ CUP (50 G) RYE FLOUR
+ EXTRA FOR THE CLOTH
5 OZ. (150 G) JASON'S BASIC
FRENCH LEVAIN
(PAGE 37)
$^1/_2$ TABLESPOON SALT
$^1/_2$ CUP (75 G) TOASTED
SUNFLOWER SEEDS
SUNFLOWER OIL FOR THE BOWL
SEMOLINA FOR THE PEEL

Make the sponge: in a large bowl whisk together the yeast and scant ½ cup (100 ml) of the warm water until the yeast has dissolved. Stir in the white flour. Cover the bowl with plastic wrap and leave in a warm place for 2 hours or until the sponge has risen by at least one-third and is clearly active, with lots of bubbles.

Put all the remaining ingredients in the bowl of a heavy-duty electric mixer fitted with the dough hook, and add the sponge. Turn the mixer on at the lowest speed and work for 8 minutes, when a rough ball of dough will have formed. Turn the speed up to medium and knead for 4 minutes. Remove the dough from the bowl and put it in a lightly oiled bowl. Cover the bowl with plastic wrap and let rise in a warm place for 1–1½ hours.

While the dough is rising, take a large dish towel or linen cloth and rub a little rye flour into the surface, then lay it, flour-side up, on a large tray.

Tip the dough out onto a lightly floured work surface and deflate it gently by tapping it out with your hands to form a rectangle. Shape into a bâton (page 27).

Place the loaf, seam-side up, on the floured cloth. Cover with another cloth and let rise at warm room temperature for 3½–4 hours.

Preheat the oven to maximum—at least 500°F—with a baking stone or heavy metal baking sheet set on the middle shelf. Dust a rimless metal cookie sheet lightly with semolina, to use as a peel.

Turn the loaf out, seam-side down, onto your hand, and transfer it seam-side down onto the side of the peel. Open the oven door and quickly slide the loaf onto the baking stone. Shut the door and get your spray bottle. Open the door again and quickly spray the sides and bottom of the oven, taking no more than 5 seconds. Shut the oven door and leave the bread to bake for 10 minutes. Lower the oven temperature to 425°F and bake the bread for a further 35–40 minutes or until it is dark brown in color (the malt in the granary flour will accentuate this) and it sounds hollow when tapped on the base.

Transfer the loaf to a wire rack to cool to room temperature before slicing.

Dan's garlic bread

This is a remarkable bread, intense in flavor without being overpowering, sweet without being sugary, each bite a complete mouthful of contrasting textures and tastes. It is beautiful to look at, both as a whole loaf and as slices on a plate. Eat it on its own or to complement a simple, lightly dressed leaf salad.

MAKES 1 LOAF

1^1/$_4$ CUPS (300 ML) WARM BOTTLED SPRING WATER (ABOUT 68°F)

3^1/$_2$ CUPS (425 G) WHITE BREAD FLOUR + EXTRA FOR DUSTING

1 PACKAGE QUICK-RISING ACTIVE DRY YEAST

^{1}/$_3$ CUP (75 ML) FRESHLY SQUEEZED ORANGE JUICE

^{2}/$_3$ CUP (100 G) "00" FLOUR

2^1/$_2$ TEASPOONS SALT

^{1}/$_3$ CUP (75 ML) EXTRA VIRGIN OLIVE OIL + EXTRA FOR BRUSHING

POLENTA FOR THE BAKING SHEET

GARLIC FILLING

3 HEADS OF GARLIC, SEPARATED INTO CLOVES

2 TABLESPOONS EXTRA VIRGIN OLIVE OIL

1–2 TABLESPOONS WATER

1 TABLESPOON BALSAMIC VINEGAR

3 TABLESPOONS SUGAR

1 TEASPOON SALT

^{1}/$_4$ TEASPOON BLACK PEPPER

1 SPRIG OF FRESH ROSEMARY, LEAVES PICKED AND CHOPPED

Warm a 4-quart mixing bowl with hot water. Pour in the bottled water, then whisk in half of the white bread flour and all the yeast. Leave in a warm place for 1 ^{1}/$_2$–2 hours or until the mixture froths.

Add the orange juice, the remaining white bread flour, the "OO" flour, and salt, then stir with your hands until the mixture forms a rough ball in the center of the bowl. The dough will be very wet and sticky: it is the high water content that helps to give the bread its open texture.

Pour one-third of the olive oil on top of the dough, and rub a little on the palms of your hands. Start to tuck the dough underneath itself. Rotate the bowl in quarter turns, turning the dough over and tucking under each time, until you have a smooth, shiny mass. Cover the bowl with plastic wrap and leave in a warm place for 45 minutes.

Lightly deflate the dough with your fingers, making dozens of indentations. Zigzag another third of the olive oil on the surface before repeating the tucking action. Re-cover the bowl with plastic wrap and leave in a warm place for 30 minutes. Repeat the deflating and tucking process, adding the remaining oil and then covering as before. Deflate and tuck five more times (without oil) at 30-minute intervals—a total of 3 hours. By the end the dough should be soft and smooth with no discernible floury lumps.

continued on next page

For the filling, blanch the garlic in boiling water for 2 minutes, refresh briefly in cold water, and peel. Put the olive oil in a small, heavy-based frying pan over a medium heat. When it shimmers, add the garlic and sauté for about a minute, being careful not to burn it. Add the water and balsamic vinegar, and, as they bubble, stir in the sugar, salt, pepper, and rosemary. Reduce the heat to its lowest setting and simmer for 5 minutes, when the garlic will be quite soft. Increase the heat and boil down the liquid until only a syrupy residue remains. Transfer the garlic to a bowl, scraping up all the syrup, and reserve.

Tip the dough out onto a floured surface and press out with the fingers and heels of your hands until you have a rectangle about 7 x 14 inches and ³/₄ inch thick (1). Spread the cooked garlic and its syrup over the surface (2). Fold the long side farthest from you across by a third (3), then take the opposite side and fold that over the first, trapping layers of filling between the folds (4). Repeat the folding action with the ends (5, 6). Flip the dough over, cover with a damp cloth, and let rest for 30 minutes.

Brush a large baking sheet with olive oil and dust with polenta. Using a sharp knife, cut the dough parcel across into 2-inch slices (7) and lay them, cut-side up, in a single layer on the sheet, stretching each slice slightly into an oval. You can keep the slices separate, to bake individual small loaves, or arrange them so they are touching, in which case you will have a "pull-apart" loaf. Cover with a damp cloth and let rise in a warm part of the kitchen for 1 hour or until almost doubled in size.

Preheat the oven to 500°F.

Brush the top of the loaf with olive oil. Spray the the bottom and sides of the oven with water, shutting the door while you get the bread. Place it, on its baking sheet, on the middle shelf. After 5 minutes, reduce the oven temperature to 350°F and bake for a further 35–40 minutes or until the loaf is quite brown and blistered, and feels firm when pressed.

Remove to a wire rack and let cool to room temperature before slicing.

6

7

Semolina-crust pain de mie

A separately yeasted semolina topping makes for a dramatic appearance on this bread. Pain de mie has a rich, soft interior, the crumb in marked contrast to the well-developed crust—a perfect sandwich loaf, and also ideal for bread and butter pudding.

MAKES 2 LOAVES

DOUGH

1 PACKAGE QUICK-RISING ACTIVE DRY YEAST

1 CUP (250 ML) WARM WHOLE MILK (ABOUT 68°F)

4^2/$_3$ CUPS (575 G) ALL-PURPOSE FLOUR + EXTRA FOR DUSTING

2^1/$_2$ TEASPOONS SALT

1^1/$_2$ TABLESPOONS SUGAR

SCANT ^{1}/$_2$ CUP (100 ML) COLD MILK (ABOUT 50°F)

3 TABLESPOONS (40 G) UNSALTED BUTTER, SOFTENED

SEMOLINA TOPPING

1^1/$_4$ CUPS (300 ML) WARM BOTTLED SPRING WATER (ABOUT 68°F)

1 PACKAGE QUICK-RISING ACTIVE DRY YEAST

1^3/$_4$ CUPS (300 G) SEMOLINA FLOUR OR GROUND RICE

3 TABLESPOONS SUNFLOWER OIL

3 TABLESPOONS (40 G) SUGAR

Make the sponge: in a large bowl whisk together the yeast and warm milk until the yeast has dissolved. Stir in 2 cups (250 g) of the flour. Cover the bowl with plastic wrap and leave in a warm place for 2 hours or until the sponge has risen by at least a third and is clearly active, with lots of bubbles.

Add the remaining flour, the salt, sugar, and cold milk to the sponge, and start to mix. With your fingertips rub in the softened butter, a little at a time, and continue mixing to form a rough dough. Transfer this to a floured work surface and knead for 10 minutes or until the dough is very soft and pliable, and its surface feels silky to the touch. Cover the dough with plastic wrap and leave on the work surface to rest for 45 minutes to 1 hour.

Meanwhile, to make the topping, pour the warm water into a bowl and whisk in the yeast until it dissolves. Add the other ingredients and mix to a smooth batter. Cover the top with plastic wrap and let rise in a warm place for 2–2^1/$_2$ hours.

Divide the dough into two pieces and shape each into a bâton (page 27).

Line a large baking sheet with a nonstick baking liner or parchment paper. Place the loaves side by side on the baking sheet, about 4 inches apart. Cover with plastic wrap and let rise in a warm place for 1^1/$_2$–2 hours or until almost doubled in bulk.

Preheat the oven to 400°F.

Discard the plastic wrap. With a skewer, lance each loaf at three points along a central line, to release any large trapped gas bubbles. Ladle the semolina topping over the loaves, smoothing and spreading the mixture with your hands so that the top surface is evenly covered.

Put the baking sheet in the center of the oven and bake for 15 minutes, then reduce the oven temperature to 350°F. Bake for a further 25–30 minutes or until the surface has cracked and blistered, and the loaves sound hollow when tapped on the base.

Remove the bread to a rack and let cool to room temperature, then remove the excess topping from the bottom edge of the bread with scissors.

Marmalade bread and butter pudding

Bread and butter pudding has been revived as a sumptuous dish, beloved by restaurateurs as the egg and cream element has increased and the bread content reduced, to produce a set custard that is equally delicious hot or cold. This is the perfect way of using up day-old Semolina-crust pain de mie (page 61), or it can be made with Brioche (page 75). If preferred, any jam can be substituted for the marmalade, although its sharp astringency cuts and balances the sweetness and richness of the pudding well.

SERVES 8

$2^{1}/_{3}$ CUPS (575 ML) MILK
$2^{1}/_{3}$ CUPS (575 ML) LIGHT OR HEAVY CREAM
1 VANILLA BEAN, SPLIT OPEN
$^{1}/_{2}$ CUP (115 G) UNSALTED BUTTER, SOFTENED
8 SLICES PAIN DE MIE OR OTHER WHITE BREAD, CRUSTS REMOVED
$^{1}/_{3}$ CUP (115 G) SEVILLE ORANGE MARMALADE
4 EGGS
2 EGG YOLKS
1 CUP (200 G) GRANULATED SUGAR
CONFECTIONERS' SUGAR FOR DUSTING

Put the milk and cream in a saucepan. Scrape the sticky black seeds from the split vanilla bean into the pan and add the bean too. Set over low heat and bring slowly to a boil. Remove from the heat and let infuse for 30 minutes.

Meanwhile, butter the slices of bread and make four marmalade sandwiches. Cut them across to make triangles and arrange in a generously buttered baking dish, slightly overlapping the triangles.

Beat the eggs and egg yolks with the granulated sugar in a bowl until they form a smooth, foaming mixture. Pour the milk and cream mixture through a strainer onto the eggs and sugar, whisking to make a smooth custard. Ladle this carefully over the bread and let soak for 30 minutes.

Preheat the oven to 325°F. Place the dish in a bain marie and pour in hot water to come halfway up the sides of the baking dish. Bake for 45 minutes or until the pudding is firm but still with some give to the gentle pressure of a finger.

Serve warm, or refrigerate overnight and serve very cold. In both cases, dust the top with confectioners' sugar before serving. Blueberries or raspberries go well with this.

FLAT BREADS AND SHAPED DOUGH

Many flat breads, such as carta musica or tortillas, do not contain yeast. The flat breads here, while raised with active yeast, are distinguished from the majority of leavened breads in that the height or thickness of the bread is deliberately restricted, with the loaves having a much larger surface area in proportion to their depth.

Roquefort and walnut fougasse

The basis for the fougasse of Provence is, in fact, a northwestern Italian flat bread. Originally a sweet bread eaten as a dessert, fougasses are now more often plain or savory. Traditionally cut into a ladder or tree shape, the slashes may also be cut through the loaf in a rough herringbone pattern.

MAKES 3 FOUGASSES

SPONGE

$3/4$ CUP (170 ML) WARM BOTTLED SPRING WATER (ABOUT 68°F)
$1^1/3$ CUPS (170 G) WHITE BREAD FLOUR
$1/2$ PACKAGE QUICK-RISING ACTIVE DRY YEAST

DOUGH AND FILLING

1 CUP + 2 TABLESPOONS (270 ML) WARM BOTTLED SPRING WATER (ABOUT 68°F)
$1/2$ PACKAGE QUICK-RISING ACTIVE DRY YEAST
$3^2/3$ CUPS (450 G) WHITE BREAD FLOUR + EXTRA FOR DUSTING
$1^1/4$ CUPS (120 G) RYE FLOUR
$2^1/2$ TEASPOONS SALT
3 TABLESPOONS EXTRA VIRGIN OLIVE OIL
7 OZ. (200 G) ROQUEFORT
$1^1/2$ CUPS (150 G) WALNUTS, TOASTED IN A 350°F OVEN AND ROUGHLY CHOPPED

Make the sponge (the fermented starter): put the water in a large bowl and mix in the flour and yeast. Keep mixing for 3–4 minutes or until a smooth batter has formed. Cover with plastic wrap and let the sponge sit in a warm place for $1^1/2$–2 hours or until it looks active and full of bubbles.

To make the dough, add the water and yeast to the sponge. Then add the flours, salt, and 1 tablespoon olive oil, and mix to a rough dough. Turn the dough out onto a floured work surface and knead for 5–8 minutes or until soft and smooth. Transfer to a clean, dry container, cover with a damp cloth, and let rise in a warm place for 30 minutes.

Return the dough to the floured work surface and pin it out into a rectangle to deflate it. Cover the surface with the crumbled Roquefort and walnuts, then gently fold the edges of the dough into the middle so that the filling is enclosed. Repeat the pinning and folding action several times. By this time the filling should be evenly distributed through the dough. (For a plain fougasse, omit the filling, but fold as described.) Transfer to a bowl, cover with plastic wrap, and let rise in a warm place for 45 minutes.

Divide the dough into three equal pieces and shape each into a ball. Leave to rest on the floured work surface, covered with a damp cloth, for 15 minutes. Then roll each piece of dough out into an oval about 10–12 inches long and 4–5 inches wide. Cut eight or nine deep slashes in each oval, cutting at an angle. Transfer the fougasses to baking sheets lined with nonstick baking liners or parchment paper, cover with plastic wrap, and let rise at room temperature for at least 1 hour.

Preheat the oven to 425°F.

Brush the fougasses with the remaining extra virgin olive oil. Bake for 15–20 minutes or until well colored, with a firm crust. The bread should sound hollow when tapped on the base. Let cool on a wire rack.

(Opposite, from top left) Roquefort and walnut fougasse, Focaccia, and Roasted pepper and paprika bread

Roasted pepper and paprika bread

Paprika, originally a Hungarian spice, is the fine powder made from a dried variety of sweet red pepper, which, although it looks like a large chili, has no heat. A similar though different-tasting spice is made in Spain where it is called pimentón. Either paprika or pimentón can be used for this recipe. It is worth investing in a good example as there are many poor quality sweet red pepper powders passed off as the real thing—if it is cheap, it is almost certainly not worth buying. Paprika and pimentón should be a dark, brick-red color and have a strong, smoky smell. If the spice is brown rather than red, it is stale and should not be used.

3 LARGE, RIPE RED BELL PEPPERS
1^1/$_2$ CUPS (370 ML) WARM
BOTTLED SPRING WATER
(ABOUT 68°F)
^{1}/$_2$ PACKAGE QUICK-RISING
ACTIVE DRY YEAST
4^3/$_4$ CUPS (575 G) WHITE BREAD
FLOUR + EXTRA FOR DUSTING
2^1/$_2$ TEASPOONS SALT
3^1/$_2$ TABLESPOONS EXTRA VIRGIN
OLIVE OIL
1 TEASPOON PAPRIKA, DISSOLVED
IN 3^1/$_2$ TABLESPOONS EXTRA
VIRGIN OLIVE OIL
SEMOLINA FOR THE BAKING SHEET

One at a time, thread the peppers onto a metal skewer and, holding the end in a cloth or oven mitt, turn over a flame until the skin blisters all over and begins to char. (If you do not have a gas range, broil the peppers, turning them frequently.) Put the peppers in a bowl and cover tightly with plastic wrap. As soon as they are cool enough to handle, strip off the skin, working from the stem end, and using a small, sharp knife to lift and pull with. Cut the peppers in half lengthwise and scrape out the seeds. Cut out the cores and white ribs. Set the peppers aside.

In the bowl of a heavy-duty electric mixer, whisk together the water, yeast, and half the flour. Cover the top of the bowl with plastic wrap and leave in a warm place for 1^1/$_2$–2 hours or until the mixture froths.

Place the remaining flour in a 4-quart bowl and add the yeast mixture, the salt, and oil. Fit the dough hook to the mixer and knead the dough for 3 minutes on a slow speed, then increase the speed to medium and briskly beat the dough for 8–9 minutes or until it is very smooth and elastic and has a satin feel. Cover the bowl with plastic wrap and let rise in a warm place for 45 minutes.

Tip the dough out onto a floured work surface. Lightly sprinkle a little flour over the surface of the dough, and rub a little more on your hands. Tap the dough out firmly with the palm and heel of your hand until it forms a rough rectangle. Fold in half, then into three in the other direction. Each time you fold, press down to remove air. Dust the bowl with flour and return the dough to it. Cover and let rise in a warm place for 30 minutes. Repeat the folding and deflating every 30 minutes for a total of 3 hours. By now the dough should be soft, aerated, and smooth.

Tip the dough out onto the floured surface. Shape it into a rough ball, leaving it seam-side down. Cover with a cloth and let rest for 15 minutes.

Flip the ball of dough over smooth-side down on the lightly floured work surface. Tap the dough out with the palms of your hands to flatten it slightly, then shape it into a bâton (page 27). Cover the dough and let rest on the work surface for 15 minutes.

Now roll out one long side of the loaf with a rolling pin, creating a rounded, flat end that extends away from the rest of the loaf and is large enough to fold back and wrap around the piece that will form the base. With your fingertips, indent the surface of the base only. Take the pepper halves and lay them over the indentations, leaving a ^{3}/$_4$-inch edge uncovered. Brush the peppers with a little of the paprika oil.

With a razor blade, slash through the rolled-out lid, creating a herringbone of cuts. Carefully lift this and wrap it over the top of the loaf, so that the peppers are slightly exposed through the lattice. Tuck around the dough so that the lattice is firmly in place. Line a heavy baking sheet with a nonstick baking liner or parchment paper and sprinkle with semolina. Transfer the loaf to the sheet. Let rise in a warm part of the kitchen for 45 minutes to 1 hour or until almost doubled in size.

Preheat the oven to 500°F.

Brush the top of the loaf with the remaining paprika oil. Bake for 15 minutes, then reduce the oven temperature to 350°F and bake for a further 30–35 minutes or until the loaf is well browned and slightly blistered, and feels firm when touched.

Remove from the baking sheet and let cool on a wire rack.

Focaccia

Focaccia is described as an Italian flat bread, a rather confusing description since it is leavened using active yeast. However, it is spread out and baked on sheets or in pans, which gives it a characteristic rectangular shape, the top marked with regular depressions. It turns a beautiful golden brown from the liberal dressing with olive oil it receives just before going in the oven. A common mistake is to incorporate too much olive oil into the dough itself, leading to a poor rise and an oily finish. Focaccia is always well salted on the surface and often includes rosemary.

MAKES 2 FOCACCIA

1 PACKAGE QUICK-RISING
ACTIVE DRY YEAST
2^1/$_2$ CUPS (680 ML) WARM
BOTTLED SPRING WATER
(ABOUT 68°F)
8 CUPS (1 KG) WHITE BREAD
FLOUR + EXTRA
FOR DUSTING
5 TEASPOONS SALT
1 TEASPOON SUGAR
1 TABLESPOON OLIVE OIL + MORE
FOR BRUSHING

TO FINISH

LEAVES FROM 2 SPRIGS OF FRESH
ROSEMARY (ABOUT 1 HEAPED
TABLESPOON), OPTIONAL
^{1}/$_3$ CUP (75 ML) EXTRA VIRGIN
OLIVE OIL
COARSE SEA SALT

Make the sponge: in a large bowl whisk together the yeast and the warm water until the yeast has dissolved. Stir in 4 cups (500 g) of the flour. Cover the bowl with plastic wrap and leave in a warm place for 2 hours or until the sponge has risen by at least one-third and is clearly active, with lots of bubbles.

Put the remaining flour in the bowl of a heavy-duty electric mixer fitted with the dough hook, and add the sponge, salt, sugar, and oil. Mixing at the lowest speed, work for 7 minutes. If the dough is too stiff, add a little more water, 1 tablespoon at a time. It should be firm and slightly sticky. Increase to full speed and beat for 1 minute, when you should have an elastic dough that is resilient to the push of a finger and that springs back when you stop pushing.

Turn out onto a floured surface and shape into a ball. Oil a bowl large enough to allow the dough to treble in size. Put the dough in and brush the top with a little more olive oil. Cover the top with plastic wrap and put to rise in a cool, draft-free place for about 2 hours. The dough will be moist, sticky, and elastic when you take it from the bowl.

Transfer to a heavily floured work surface. Tap the dough out firmly with the palm and heel of your hand until it forms a rough rectangle. Fold in half, then into three in the other direction, until the dough is folded like a blanket. Divide it in half, and tap and press out each piece into a rectangle again. Transfer to two floured nonstick jellyroll pans, each measuring about 8 x 12 inches, and push out to fill the pans evenly. Cover each pan with a cloth and let rise at room temperature for 1 hour.

Preheat the oven to 500°F.

With the tips of your fingers, poke holes in the dough to dimple the surfaces comprehensively in straight lines. Sprinkle on the rosemary, if using. Zigzag the olive oil over and scatter coarse salt on top. Bake in the center of the oven for 10 minutes, then turn the temperature down to 400°F. Continue baking for 15–20 minutes, when the focaccia will have risen to a height of about 2 inches. Remove and let cool in the pans. To serve, cut in squares.

Rolled out to thin rounds, focaccia dough is perfect as a pizza base. Keep toppings to a minimum— the best pizzas have the most basic and simple toppings, like a classic margherita of tomato, mozzarella, and basil. For baking pizzas, a very hot oven and a baking stone are ideal, though metal pizza pans also work well. Allow about 8 minutes in the oven.

Pretzels

Our pretzels are big, New York-style twists of pagnotta dough dusted with sesame seeds or zahtar, baked golden crisp but with a nicely light-textured crumb. Zahtar is a Middle Eastern spice mix given a characteristic sour edge by sumac, which is a red powder made from the dried berries of a shrub of that name. Sumac is used extensively in Iraqi cooking. To make zahtar, mix together equal amounts of powdered sumac and ground dried marjoram and thyme.

MAKES 1 BIG PRETZEL

7 OZ. (200 G) PAGNOTTA DOUGH
(PAGE 39) OR FOCACCIA
DOUGH (PAGE 68), RISEN
AND READY TO SHAPE
WHITE BREAD FLOUR FOR
DUSTING
SUNFLOWER OIL AND SEMOLINA
FOR THE PEEL

TO FINISH
1 EGG
1 TABLESPOON WATER
1–2 TEASPOONS ZAHTAR OR
SESAME SEEDS

On a heavily floured surface, roll the dough into a cylinder about 20 inches long. Turn this to make a loop, as if making the first move when tying a tie. You will have an oval with one piece of dough crossing over itself, like a lapel ribbon. Twist the loop in the middle to give two equal loops above the crossed-over tails of the dough. Bring the tails up and over the loops, pressing down.

Flour a cloth-lined tray. Transfer the pretzel to the tray. Cover with another cloth and let rise in a warm place for 30 minutes.

Preheat the oven to 425°F, with a baking stone or heavy metal baking sheet on the middle rack. Lightly brush a rimless metal cookie sheet with oil and dust with semolina: this will act as a peel.

During the rise the pretzel will have contracted as well as expanded. Tug and stretch it gently to restore its shape. Transfer to the peel. Lightly beat the egg with the water and brush this over the pretzel. Scatter the zahtar or sesame seeds on top. Slide the pretzel onto the baking stone and bake for 40–45 minutes.

Remove to a wire rack to cool.

Grissini

Grissini—crisp bread sticks—were first made in Turin, Italy, and remain a specialty of that city's small street bakeries. They bear little resemblance to mass-produced grissini, which are machine-made, identical, smooth, and snapping to a tongue-drying dust in the mouth. Turin's grissini are closer to loaves, and some are up to a yard long.

MAKES ABOUT 25 GRISSINI (ABOUT 10 INCHES LONG)

1 RECIPE PAGNOTTA DOUGH (PAGE 39) OR FOCACCIA DOUGH (PAGE 68), RISEN AND READY TO SHAPE
WHITE BREAD FLOUR FOR DUSTING
SEMOLINA FOR DUSTING

TO FINISH (OPTIONAL)
1/4 CUP (60 ML) EXTRA VIRGIN OLIVE OIL
CHOPPED FRESH THYME, ROSEMARY, OR OREGANO
3 TABLESPOONS COARSE SEA SALT
COARSELY GROUND BLACK PEPPER

On a floured work surface flatten the dough out with your hands. Lightly flour the surface of the dough, then roll out with a rolling pin into a long rectangle, as thin as you can. The dough will reach a point when it resists your best efforts and shrinks back. When this happens, cover it with a dish towel and let it rest for 15–20 minutes. Then resume rolling, resting the dough, covered, a second time. On the third rolling you should have a rectangle about $^3/_8$ inch thick.

Line two baking sheets with nonstick baking liners or parchment paper and sprinkle with semolina. With a sharp knife, roughly cut the dough rectangle into $^1/_2$-inch-wide lengths. Make lengthwise cuts in one end of each strip of dough, if you like. Transfer them as you cut to the baking sheets, leaving space between them. When you have used up all the dough, cover the trays with plastic wrap and let rise at warm room temperature for 45 minutes to 1 hour.

Preheat the oven to 400°F. If you like, you can lightly brush the tops of the grissini with a little olive oil, then sprinkle them with a few chopped herbs, coarse sea salt, or black pepper. At Baker & Spice the grissini are kept plain, covered only with a light dusting of flour.

Place the baking sheets in the oven and bake for 20–30 minutes or until the grissini are lightly colored and crisp. Once removed from the oven, transfer to a wire rack to cool.

SWEET YEASTED BAKING

The tradition of baking sweet yeasted doughs enriched with eggs and butter is almost as old as leavened bread. The products can range from relatively simple spice breads with festive calendar associations, like hot cross buns and pain d'épices, to sophisticated and luxurious brioches.

Hot cross buns

Sweet, moist, spicy, and studded with fruit, hot cross buns are that British rarity—a seasonally baked specialty. Of course they are just as nice without their piped Easter cross at any time of the year.

Makes 24 buns

1 package quick-rising active dry yeast
scant 1 cup (200 ml) warm bottled spring water (about 68°F)
7 cups (870 g) white bread flour + extra for dusting
1 cup (230 ml) cold bottled spring water (about 50°F)
3¹/₂ tablespoons (25 g) nonfat dry milk
¹/₂ cup (100 g) sugar
4 teaspoons salt
6 tablespoons (85 g) unsalted butter, softened
1 egg
¹/₃ cup (40 g) apple-pie spice
²/₃ cup (100 g) raisins
1 cup (150 g) mixed diced dried apricots and candied peel

Piping paste and glazes
¹/₄ cup (35 g) all-purpose flour
¹/₂ cup (100 g) + 1 tablespoon sugar
1 egg yolk
1 tablespoon milk

Make the sponge: in a large bowl whisk together the yeast and the warm water until the yeast has dissolved. Stir in 1¹/₂ cups (200 g) of the flour. Cover the bowl with plastic wrap and leave in a warm place for 2 hours or until the sponge has risen by at least one-third and is clearly active, with lots of bubbles.

Put the remaining flour in the bowl of a heavy-duty electric mixer fitted with the dough hook, and add the sponge, cold water, nonfat dry milk, sugar, salt, butter, egg, and spice. Switch on at the lowest speed and work for 8 minutes, when you will have a very soft dough. Add the apricots and peel, turn up the speed to medium, and knead for 1 minute only. Remove the dough to a floured work surface and knead for 1 minute, then form a ball. Put into a bowl, cover with plastic wrap, and let rise in a warm place for 45 minutes to 1 hour or until doubled in bulk.

Turn out onto the lightly floured work surface and gently press out into a rectangle to deflate. Divide into 24 equal pieces, preferably using scales to be precise. Form each piece into a neat ball. Line baking sheets with nonstick baking liners or parchment paper, and arrange the balls on the sheets in lines, almost but not quite touching. Cover with a slightly damp cloth and let rise in a warm place for 45 minutes or until the buns have doubled in size and joined together as they have expanded.

Halfway through the rise, preheat the oven to 500°F. Make the piping paste for the crosses by mixing the flour and 1 tablespoon sugar with 1 tablespoon cold water. Put into a pastry bag fitted with a small, plain tip. Beat the egg yolk and milk together for a glaze.

Using a skewer or a blunt knife, indent a cross on the top of each bun. Brush with the egg glaze, then pipe a cross in the indentation. Put the buns in the oven, turning the temperature down to 350°F as soon as you shut the door. Bake for 30–40 minutes or until the buns are golden and darkening around the outside edges. Like bread rolls, they will sound hollow when tapped on the base.

Transfer to a wire rack. Dissolve the ¹/₂ cup (100 g) sugar in 3 tablespoons water and bring to a boil. Brush this glaze over the buns. Resist the temptation to pull them apart until they have cooled to room temperature.

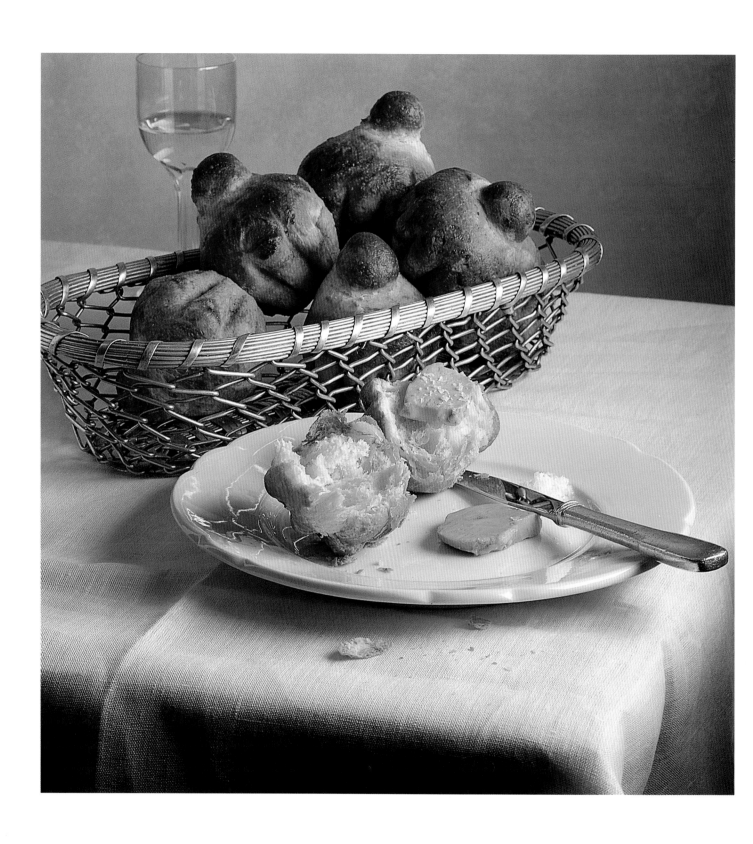

Brioche

Brioche is the most luxurious of breads, made rich and yellow with butter and eggs. This enrichment gives it a close texture, more like a cake than a bread. It is usually eaten at breakfast, but when sliced and toasted also forms the classic accompaniment to a foie gras terrine.

Some brioche recipes are very rich, with equal parts flour and butter, but you will get a more consistent result using half the weight of butter to flour.

MAKES 2 LARGE BRIOCHES OR 16 INDIVIDUAL BRIOCHES

1 PACKAGE QUICK-RISING ACTIVE DRY YEAST
4 CUPS (500 G) WHITE BREAD FLOUR + EXTRA FOR DUSTING
¼ CUP (60 ML) WARM BOTTLED SPRING WATER (ABOUT 68°F)
4 TEASPOONS SALT
6 TABLESPOONS (75 G) SUGAR
5 EGGS
1 CUP + 2 TABLESPOONS (250 G) UNSALTED BUTTER, SOFTENED

GLAZE
2 EGG YOLKS
2 TABLESPOONS MILK OR WATER

Make the sponge: dissolve the yeast and ¼ cup (25 g) of the flour in the warm water. Cover and leave in a warm place for 30–40 minutes or until bubbling and clearly active.

Place the remaining flour in the bowl of a heavy-duty electric mixer fitted with the paddle, and add the sponge, salt, sugar, and eggs. Mix at low speed until the dough comes together, about 7 minutes. Add the butter, increase the mixer speed to medium, and continue to mix for about 15 minutes, when the butter will be fully incorporated and the dough will be shiny and elastic. Transfer the dough to a plastic container or bowl, cover tightly, and refrigerate overnight.

Put the dough on a floured work surface. Divide it in half, or into 16 pieces weighing 2 oz. (60 g) each (for individual brioches). Shape each piece into a ball and let rest for 20 minutes.

For each large brioche: divide the ball of dough into two pieces, one about one-third of the total amount. Shape the larger piece of dough into a ball, then make a hole in the center of the top with your finger and push down until you break through the bottom. Stretch the hole with your fingers until you have a rather fat and tall ring doughnut. Now shape the smaller piece into a cylinder tapered at one end. Cut through the tapered end from its end to halfway up. You should have a shape that looks a little like a tooth, with the split tapered end forming its roots. Place this end into the hole in the doughnut, pulling the roots through and tucking them under the base. This will ensure that the head of the brioche rises straight up, and does not lean to one side. Tuck the top edge of the doughnut back into the hole; this will keep the two pieces together as the brioche rises.

For each individual brioche: using the edge of your outstretched hand like a knife, make an indentation in the ball of dough to measure off about one-third of the diameter. Lightly grip the large end of the dough ball with your other hand, and rock the dough back and forth, separating a smaller ball joined by a thread to the larger ball. Then carefully turn the large ball upright and shove your fingers into the top to make an indentation. Place the smaller ball of dough into it, coiling the joining thread underneath into the hole.

Lightly brush two fluted brioche molds (or 16 individual molds) with melted butter and dust over that with a little flour. Place the shaped brioches firmly inside the molds. Let rise in a warm place for 3–4 hours or until doubled in bulk.

Preheat the oven to 400°F.

For the glaze, lightly beat the egg yolks with the milk or water. Brush the top of the brioches with the glaze. Bake for 10–15 minutes, then reduce the heat to 350°F. For large brioches, bake for a further 35–40 minutes, or 15–20 minutes for individual ones, or until risen and a good golden brown.

Fig and brioche tart

The amount of filling here may seem inadequate, but the brioche dough swells and rises so much it would squeeze any larger amount out. The tart is best on the day of baking.

MAKES AN 8½-INCH TART

8 OZ. (250 G) BRIOCHE DOUGH
(PAGE 75), RISEN AND
READY TO SHAPE
7–8 FRESH, RIPE FIGS
¼ CUP (60 G) PLAIN LOW-FAT
YOGURT
5 TABLESPOONS (60 G) SUGAR
¼ CUP (60 ML) HEAVY CREAM
4 EGG YOLKS
GRATED ZEST OF ½ LEMON
2½ TEASPOONS CORNSTARCH

Preheat the oven to 350°F.

Roll the brioche dough out to a thickness of ¼ inch and use to line a lightly oiled 8½-inch fluted round tart pan that is 1 inch deep, preferably one with a removable bottom. Take the halved figs and place them, cut-side up and slightly overlapping, on the dough. Put all the remaining ingredients in a bowl and mix thoroughly. Pour this custard over and around the figs.

Place in the oven and bake for 15 minutes. Reduce the oven temperature to 300°F and bake for a further 35–40 minutes or until the brioche is risen and golden brown, and the filling just set. Check after 25 minutes—if it looks as if it is browning too quickly, cover it with a small sheet of foil.

Let cool to room temperature and then serve.

Prune clafoutis

Clafoutis, which comes from Limousin in central France, originally featured the tiny black cherries the region is famous for. The dessert is also often made with halved plums or apricots when they are at their seasonal best. Prunes are available all year round and, enlivened with a little brandy and sugar, make a particularly good clafoutis. The best prunes to use are from Agen, France, though if you cannot get these, California prunes are also very good.

A clafoutis is traditionally made without pastry, but the batter can be baked in a sweet pastry shell (page 131) to make a delicious and different tart that is delicious with whipped cream.

SERVES 6

14 OZ. (400 G) PITTED PRUNES
SCANT ¼ CUP (50 ML) BRANDY
¼ CUP (50 G) SUGAR

BATTER
¾ CUP (125 G) ALL-PURPOSE
FLOUR
⅔ CUP (150 ML) WHOLE MILK
¼ CUP (60 ML) HEAVY CREAM
2 TABLESPOONS (30 G)
UNSALTED BUTTER
2 EGGS
¼ CUP (50 G) SUGAR

If using prunes that need to be rehydrated, put to soak overnight in an infusion of weak, sugared tea. Drain, then put back in the bowl, add the brandy and sugar, and toss to coat evenly. Let macerate for 2–3 hours at room temperature.

Preheat the oven to 350°F. Grease an 8 x 12-inch baking dish with butter, then dust lightly with flour and reserve.

Sift the flour into a bowl. In a pan, heat the milk and cream together until hot but not boiling. Remove from the heat and add the butter, then leave it to melt.

With a portable electric mixer or whisk, beat the eggs and sugar together until pale and creamy, then add the milk mixture. Stir in gently with a spoon. Fold in the flour to make a smooth, soft batter. Do not beat hard as this would toughen the cooked mixture and affect the rise.

Drain the prunes and distribute them evenly in the prepared dish. Pour the batter over. Bake for 40–45 minutes or until the batter has risen up around the prunes and the surface has a nice golden color.

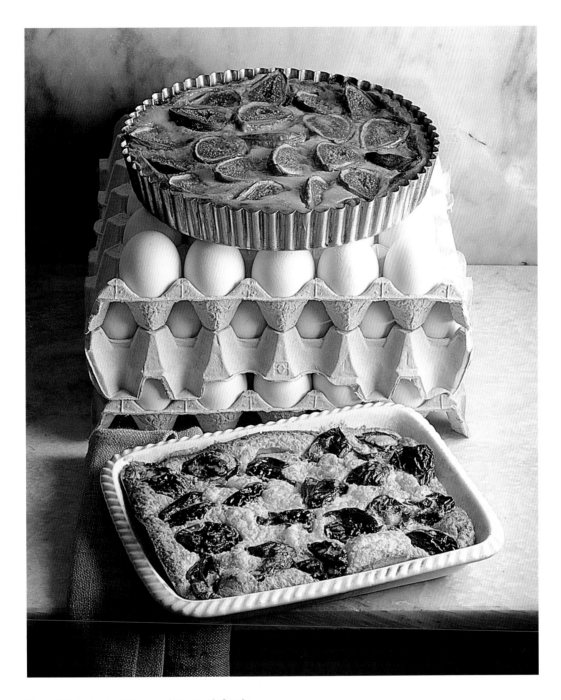

Fig and brioche tart, top, and Prune clafoutis

Crumpets

Crumpets have been an English teatime favorite since the early seventeenth century. Then they were made from buckwheat flour, which makes them sound similar to blinis, the small Russian yeast pancakes served with caviar. In 1769, Elizabeth Raffald described crumpets made with wheat flour in a batter raised with a sourdough starter, cooked on a griddle before being toasted before an open fire. The crumpet's popularity reached its zenith in the 1920s and '30s, when afternoon tea would not have been complete without hot buttered crumpets and jam.

Crumpets are traditionally cooked on a flat griddle, though you can also use a heavy-based frying pan or a nonstick pan. Difficulties may come from using too much yeast, from having too solid a batter, or from cooking at the wrong temperature. To make crumpets properly you will need some 3½-inch metal crumpet or muffin rings (or straight-sided metal pastry cutters) to put on the flat metal surface on which you cook them.

MAKES 12 CRUMPETS

3 CUPS (450 G) ALL-PURPOSE FLOUR
1 TEASPOON SUGAR
1 PACKAGE QUICK-RISING ACTIVE DRY YEAST
1½ CUPS (350 ML) SKIM MILK
1½ CUPS (350 ML) BOTTLED SPRING WATER
1 TEASPOON SALT
½ TEASPOON BAKING SODA
SUNFLOWER OIL FOR COOKING

Sift the flour into a bowl with the sugar and yeast. Warm the skim milk and water to about 68°F, then use a whisk to beat this liquid into the flour to make a smooth batter. Cover the bowl with plastic wrap and let stand at room temperature for about 2 hours. The batter will more than double in size before falling slightly.

Beat in the salt and baking soda. Let rest for 10 minutes while you heat a griddle or heavy frying pan over a low flame.

You must now judge whether your batter is the right consistency, which should be like that of light cream. If too thick, the honeycomb of holes, which is the defining point of the crumpet, will not occur. If too thin, the batter will run from under the rings. If the cooking surface is too hot, the batter will burn before the crumpet is ready to be turned; if too cool, the crumpet will rise incompletely and be leaden. Test both batter and heat of pan by cooking a spoonful of batter before proceeding. If the batter is too thick, thin with a little water; if too thin, beat in a little more flour.

Moisten a piece of paper towel with oil and rub over the inside of the metal rings and the hot surface of the griddle, placing the rings on top. Put 3 tablespoons of batter into each ring. Cook for 6–8 minutes or until the surface is set and filled with holes. Turn the crumpets and rings over with a metal spatula and cook for a further 2–3 minutes. The first side should be a chestnut brown, the second only barely colored, and the crumpets about 1¼ inches thick. Lift off the rings with a cloth. Eat at once, or let cool and then toast the pale side. Serve with butter and jam or honey.

Doughnuts

The two keys to successful doughnuts are a properly risen sweet yeast dough and clean oil at the right temperature. This is 375°F, the temperature at which the exterior of the doughnut is sealed, preventing excessive fat absorption, and hot enough to cause the carbon dioxide gas trapped inside the dough to expand rapidly, giving the right, airy light texture. Frying a yeasted dough gives a completely different exterior finish to baking and a lovely, uniform golden brown color. Before you begin, change the oil in the fryer and clean the interior. Any neutral-tasting oil, like sunflower, will do.

MAKES 20 DOUGHNUTS

1 PACKAGE QUICK-RISING
ACTIVE DRY YEAST
$^3/_4$ CUP (175 ML) WARM MILK
(ABOUT 68°F)
3 CUPS (450 G) ALL-PURPOSE
FLOUR + EXTRA FOR DUSTING
1 TEASPOON SALT
6 TABLESPOONS (85 G) UNSALTED
BUTTER, DICED AND SOFTENED
2 EGGS, BEATEN
7 TABLESPOONS (85 G) SUGAR
+ EXTRA FOR COATING
GRATED ZEST OF 1 LEMON
1 TEASPOON GROUND CINNAMON
SUNFLOWER OIL FOR BRUSHING
OIL FOR DEEP FRYING

Make the sponge: in a large bowl whisk together the yeast and the warm milk until the yeast has dissolved. Stir in 1$^1/_4$ cups (170 g) of the flour. Cover the bowl with plastic wrap and leave in a warm place for 2 hours or until the sponge has risen by at least one-third and is clearly active, with lots of bubbles.

Put the remaining flour in the bowl of a heavy-duty electric mixer fitted with the dough hook, and add the sponge and salt. Turn on at the lowest speed. Add the butter one piece at a time. When fully incorporated, add the beaten eggs, one at a time. Add the sugar, grated lemon zest, and cinnamon, and knead for 8 minutes. Turn to full speed and knead for a further 2 minutes.

Turn the sticky dough out onto a heavily floured surface and finish kneading by hand, incorporating additional flour until you have a smooth, elastic ball of dough. Brush this with a little oil and place in a lightly oiled bowl. Cover with plastic wrap. Let rise at room temperature for 2 hours or until at least doubled in size.

Turn the dough onto the floured surface and gently press out to a rectangle. Divide into 20 equal pieces, rolling them into balls. If you want to make ring doughnuts, make a hole in the center of each ball by pushing your finger through, then circle your finger to enlarge the hole to about $^3/_4$-inch diameter. Put the doughnuts on a floured tray and cover with a cloth. Let rise in a warm place for 40–50 minutes or until doubled in size.

Heat oil for deep frying to 375°F. Fry the doughnuts in small batches, being careful not to overcrowd the pan as this will cause the temperature of the oil to drop below sealing point. Fry for 1–2 minutes on the first side, then turn and give them a further minute on the other side. When done, drain on paper towels.

Put some sugar on a plate and turn the doughnuts in this to coat while still warm. Serve as soon as possible—they are best eaten minutes from the pan.

Plum fritters

Fritters can be savory or sweet. They are made either by mixing chopped elements into a fairly thick batter or by dipping larger pieces into a thinner, coating batter. In both cases they are deep-fried. Our fritters are filled with seasonal fruit, and the dough is quite wet so it molds around the fruit easily. Ripe plums make great fritters, although they can be made using a variety of fruit—really anything that is not too juicy. Fritters are best enjoyed still warm, and certainly never more than 2 hours from their frying.

Amounts for the dough can be doubled, but if you do this, still use the same amount of yeast.

MAKES 10 FRITTERS

1^1/$_4$ CUPS (300 ML) WARM
BOTTLED SPRING WATER
(ABOUT 68°F)
1 PACKAGE QUICK-RISING
ACTIVE DRY YEAST
2^1/$_3$ CUPS (300 G) ALL-PURPOSE
FLOUR + EXTRA FOR DUSTING
1^1/$_2$ TABLESPOONS SUGAR
+ EXTRA FOR DREDGING
GRATED ZEST OF 1 LEMON
1 TEASPOON SALT
5 RIPE PLUMS
OIL FOR DEEP-FRYING

Put the warm water in the bowl of a heavy-duty electric mixer fitted with the dough hook. Add the yeast and switch on at low speed, then add all the remaining ingredients except the plums. Work for 10 minutes to produce a shiny, thick batter. Alternatively, make the batter using a whisk. Cover the top of the bowl with plastic wrap and let rise in a warm place for 2 hours.

Heat oil for deep frying to 375°F.

Cut the plums in half and discard the pits. Add the plums to the batter and fold them in. With a large metal spoon, scoop out one batter-coated plum half and lower it gently into the hot oil. Add another three batter-coated plums to the pan, keeping them separate, then fry for 4–5 minutes, turning the fritters over halfway through. They will expand and set, and turn golden brown. Remove with a slotted spoon to paper towels to drain. Dredge with sugar and serve as soon as possible, frying the remaining fritters in small batches in the same way.

When deep-frying, strict adherence to a few essential rules will guarantee perfect results. The oil used should be neutral in flavor and capable of sustaining a temperature of 375°F—sealing heat—without burning. Peanut, canola, sunflower, and corn oil are all suitable. Using clean oil is also very important. Ideally, the oil should be fresh each time you fry, but certainly changed after no more than three uses. Frying crumbed items degrades the oil fastest. The pan should be no more than half full of oil, and you can check the temperature with a deep-frying thermometer.

Krantz cake

Yeast cakes are a feature of German baking, and this one is filled typically with a walnut and chocolate mixture. It could also have a more spicy, Middle Eastern filling that includes poppy seeds. The recipe was given to Ilan Schwartz by his mother. He cooked it for us when he was head of our *Viennoiserie*.

MAKES 2 CAKES

1 PACKAGE QUICK-RISING ACTIVE DRY YEAST
4 CUPS (500 G) WHITE BREAD FLOUR
1 TABLESPOON WARM BOTTLED SPRING WATER (ABOUT 68°F)
^{2}/3 CUP (150 G) CREAM CHEESE
^{2}/3 CUP (150 G) SOUR CREAM
^{3}/4 CUP (150 G) SUGAR
^{2}/3 CUP (150 G) UNSALTED BUTTER, MELTED
4 EGG YOLKS
PINCH OF SALT
SUNFLOWER OIL FOR THE BOWL

FILLING
^{1}/2 CUP (100 G) SUGAR
1 CUP (100 G) WALNUT HALVES
4 OZ. (100 G) BITTERSWEET CHOCOLATE

GLAZES
1 EGG YOLK
1 TABLESPOON MILK
^{1}/4 CUP (50 G) SUGAR
^{1}/4 CUP (60 ML) BOTTLED SPRING WATER

In a small bowl mix together the yeast, 2 tablespoons of the flour, and the warm water. Cover and leave in a warm place for about 2 hours or until the yeast begins to show signs of activity and starts to bubble.

Put the cream cheese, sour cream, sugar, melted butter, and egg yolks in the bowl of a heavy-duty electric mixer fitted with the whisk. Beat together, then add the yeast batter and the remaining flour. Beat on a medium speed for 5–6 minutes, adding the salt as the mixture combines. The dough will be very sticky and difficult to handle. Transfer to a lightly oiled bowl, cover with plastic wrap, and leave in the refrigerator overnight.

The next day, remove the dough from the refrigerator 20–30 minutes before you start working with it. Oil two 2-pound loaf pans.

Make the filling: put the sugar and walnuts in a food processor and blitz to a fine crumb. Transfer to a bowl. Roughly chop the chocolate with a knife, and mix with the sugar and walnuts.

On a lightly floured surface, roll out the dough into a rectangle about ^{1}/4 inch thick. Spread with the filling and roll up like a jelly roll, starting from a long side. With a sharp knife, cut through the roll lengthwise and separate the two pieces. Twist them together loosely, keeping the cut sides up, then cut the twisted loaf across in half. Drop each piece into a prepared loaf pan. Cover with a cloth and let rise in a warm place for 1^1/2–2 hours or until doubled in bulk.

Preheat the oven to 350°F.

Beat the egg yolk and milk together and brush over the cakes. Bake for 15 minutes, then lower the oven temperature to 325°F and bake for a further 25–30 minutes or until well colored.

Just before the cakes come out of the oven, make the sugar glaze: dissolve the sugar in the water and bring just to a boil. Brush the hot glaze over the cakes while they are still hot, then let them cool in the pans for 10 minutes. Unmold onto a wire rack to cool completely.

QUICK BREADS

"Quick" breads are distinguished by their use of baking powder, baking soda, and cream of tartar to generate the carbon dioxide that lightens and lifts the loaf instead of yeast. Baking soda produces a crisper finish than baking powder, which is a mixture of baking soda and cream of tartar. In our recipes we often use both baking powder and soda to deliver a perfect texture in a bread, cake, or cookie.

Cornbread

Cornbread is an all-American favorite. In the southern states of the U.S., it is traditionally flavored with bacon fat, but you can use butter, lard, or even olive oil to good effect. You can also stir various things into the batter to give the bread a different character—crisp pieces of bacon, for example, or fried onions, blanched corn kernels, or, as here, some hot chili and scallions.

SERVES 6

$^1/_2$ CUP (120 ML) MILK
6$^1/_2$ TABLESPOONS (90 G) UNSALTED BUTTER
2 CUPS (240 G) CORNMEAL
1$^2/_3$ CUPS (240 G) ALL-PURPOSE FLOUR
2 TEASPOONS BAKING POWDER
2 TEASPOONS BAKING SODA
1 TEASPOON SALT
1 EGG
$^1/_2$ CUP (120 G) PLAIN LOW-FAT YOGURT OR BUTTERMILK
1 FRESH HOT GREEN CHILI, FINELY SHREDDED
2 SCALLIONS, THINLY SLICED

Preheat the oven to 350°F. Butter an 8-inch round, deep cake pan and line the bottom with buttered parchment paper.

Warm the milk in a small pan, then remove from the heat and add the butter. Leave to melt off the heat. Sift the dry ingredients into a mixing bowl. Beat the egg with the yogurt and the buttery milk. Stir in the chili and scallions, then fold this mixture into the dry ingredients.

Pour the mixture into the prepared pan. Bake for about 25 minutes or until the top is golden and the bread firm to the touch.

Unmold and cut into wedges while still hot.

Cornbreads should always be eaten warm and taste nicest when generously buttered. They are particularly good with fried and grilled foods, such as chicken and spareribs, and with barbecue. In the South they are traditionally made in a heavy iron skillet.

Hush puppies, jonnycakes and spoon bread are other types of cornbread, all of them made from a cornmeal batter.

Whole-wheat soda bread

White soda bread

Buttermilk—originally the slightly sour residue of milk after churning to make butter—is today made commercially by adding a bacteria to skim or lowfat milk. Buttermilk gives a rich and distinctive tang to this bread, and works with baking soda to produce the carbon dioxide bubbles that make the bread rise. Plain low-fat yogurt can be substituted for the buttermilk, if you prefer.

MAKES 1 LOAF

3 CUPS (450 G) ALL-PURPOSE FLOUR
1 TEASPOON SUGAR
1 TEASPOON SALT
1 TEASPOON BAKING SODA
1 TEASPOON CREAM OF TARTAR
1½ CUPS (350 ML) BUTTERMILK

Preheat the oven to 450°F.

Sift the flour into a bowl with the sugar, salt, soda, and cream of tartar. Make a well in the center. Pour in the buttermilk, mixing with one hand and working in from the side of the bowl, while turning the bowl with the other hand. The dough should be soft but not too wet and sticky. If it is too dry to hold, add a little more buttermilk.

As soon as it holds, turn out onto a lightly floured surface and knead briefly. Shape into a ball and set on a floured baking sheet. Cut a deep cross into the top of the loaf, taking the cuts all the way through to the bottom.

Bake in the middle of the oven for 15 minutes, then turn the oven temperature down to 400°F. Continue to bake for 30 minutes, when the bread should sound hollow when tapped on the base.

Whole-wheat soda bread

An altogether gutsier presentation than the white version, the wheat germ and molasses give this bread a lot of flavor and moistness. It keeps a little better than the white soda bread, but is still best eaten fresh from the oven.

Soda bread is a great Irish tradition and should not be thought of as a tea cake. On the contrary, this bread is excellent with oysters or butter and cheese.

MAKES 1 LOAF

1¼ CUPS (300 ML) BUTTERMILK
1 TABLESPOON MOLASSES
1½ CUPS (220 G) SELF-RISING FLOUR
1¾ CUPS (220 G) WHOLE-WHEAT FLOUR
1 TABLESPOON WHEAT GERM
½ TEASPOON CREAM OF TARTAR
1 TEASPOON BAKING SODA
1 TEASPOON SALT

Preheat the oven to 375°F.

Warm the buttermilk with the molasses in a small saucepan until the molasses is very liquid. Combine all the dry ingredients in a mixing bowl. Pour in the milk and molasses mixture, and mix well with your hands to make a dough. It should be soft but not too wet and sticky. Add a little more flour if necessary.

Shape into a ball and place on a floured baking sheet. Cut a deep cross into the top of the loaf, taking the cuts all the way through to the bottom. Bake for 1 hour or until the bread sounds hollow when tapped on the base.

Scones

The secret of a good moist scone that is also light is in the proportion of leavening agent to flour. Use too much leavening and your scone will stand tall, but it will taste horribly of the baking powder chemicals. It is also important to keep the kneading to an absolute minimum or the gluten in the flour gets over-worked, which makes the dough elastic and consequently the baked scone hard.

MAKES 16 SCONES

3 CUPS (450 G) SELF-RISING
FLOUR
PINCH OF SALT
2 TABLESPOONS SUGAR + EXTRA
FOR SPRINKLING
2 TEASPOONS BAKING POWDER
6 TABLESPOONS (85 G) UNSALTED
BUTTER, SOFTENED
2 EGGS
SCANT 1 CUP (200 ML) COLD MILK
1/2 CUP (85 G) GOLDEN RAISINS
(OPTIONAL)

GLAZE
1 EGG YOLK
1 TABLESPOON MILK

Preheat the oven to 300°F. Line a large baking sheet with a nonstick baking liner or parchment paper.

Sift the flour, salt, sugar, and baking powder into a bowl. Cut the butter into small cubes and rub into the flour with your hands. Lightly beat the eggs, then add the cold milk. Pour all of the eggy milk mixture into the flour, then mix quickly and lightly together, adding the raisins if you wish. Do not work the dough too much—the quicker and lighter you are, the better the scones will be.

Tip the dough onto a lightly floured surface and roll out to a thickness of 1 inch. With a 3-inch round cutter, cut out 16 scones and put them 2 inches apart on the prepared baking sheet.

Lightly beat the egg yolk with the milk for the glaze. Brush over the tops of the scones, then sprinkle with a little sugar. Bake in the center of the oven for 20–25 minutes or until risen and lightly browned. Let cool on a wire rack, then split and fill with jam and clotted or whipped cream.

On baking bread

"A loaf can look great and have a good texture, but if it is underseasoned or does not taste right then it is a pointless exercise. There are no short cuts to baking good bread. The process is very complex, with so many variables over which you have no control. For example, you need to take the temperature of the dough coming out of the mixer, because if the ambient temperature has pushed it up higher than is desirable you have to chill the water going into the next batch to compensate.

"Bread is a living thing, and you have to love and respect it. Only when you do can your bread move from being good to being remarkable. You must believe in what you are doing. If you do not, there is not enough information in the world to make the magic happen." JASON WARWICK, HEAD BAKER

Cakes and cookies

Cakes have from ancient Greek times been both symbolic and special, roles that they continue to play to this day. There are cakes for christenings, wedding celebrations, religious days, and festive occasions. The word "cake" now describes a baked, flour-based construction, usually raised with chemical leavening agents and invariably sweet. The texture is immediately identifiable as cake, and it is distinctively different from bread. This distinction was not always apparent, however, the earliest bread being unleavened and consequently described literally as a cake. The first sweetening of this bread-cake was with honey, but in an age when sweetness did not imply that something should be eaten separately from savory dishes.

Sweetened yeast breads were probably the first cakes in the modern sense, though the cakes we eat today only started to exist with the introduction of baking powders used in conjunction with soft flour batters. Today cakes, and cookies, are treats and culminations. And they are a central part of that great British institution, afternoon tea.

CAKES

Virtually all cakes are made from soft, low-gluten flour, butter, eggs, and sugar, their respective proportions and the method of their incorporation defining the texture of the cake when baked. After that, what makes each cake individual is a matter of shape, flavorings used, and how it is iced, filled, and decorated.

The relative proportions of the base ingredients also determine the most appropriate technique to shape a cake's construction. Thus, a high percentage of butter points to "creaming" at the outset, where the butter is vigorously whipped or beaten with sugar until it becomes pale and absorbs air from the beating action, the air being the element that ensures a light texture when the cake is baked. A cake made with lots of eggs—a classic sponge—begins by whisking them with sugar, and results in a baked finish that literally springs back when gently pressed. Cakes with high levels of molasses, honey, or chocolate start with these being warmed or melted, thereby making it possible to integrate them with the other primary ingredients.

Cake batters are raised or leavened using chemicals rather than yeast. The most common of these leavening agents are baking soda and baking powder (of which baking soda is the main active ingredient). Chemical leavening agents only generate gas briefly, which is why they are unsuitable for lifting breads, which need a sustained and lengthy leavening. It is the difference in gluten levels between hard or bread flours and soft or cake flours that makes bread and cake texturally so different.

When baking soda, an alkali, is mixed with an acid, a chemical reaction is kick-started and carbon dioxide is given off. Baking soda can therefore only be used on its own to lift a batter if a suitable natural acid is present. This might be something like lactic acid, which is contained in yogurt and buttermilk, or citric acid, or molasses.

Baking powder is a complete leavening agent that only needs water to make it work. It consists of a mixture of baking soda and acid salts, with ground starch included to absorb moisture from the air. It is this inert "buffer" of starch (usually cornstarch) that prevents premature activation in the can in humid conditions.

"Double-acting" baking powder contains two different types of water-soluble salt crystals that are triggered sequentially. The first, typically cream of tartar, reacts with moisture at room temperature and initiates a reaction with the baking soda, instantly giving off little bubbles of carbon dioxide. A second acid salt crystal, usually sodium aluminum sulphate, activates only at high temperature, in the oven, generating a larger amount of carbon dioxide. The moist solids of the cake batter dry during cooking and set around the bubbles before the gas generation stops, producing a light yet moist cake.

Self-rising flour includes baking powder sufficient to raise most cakes, scones, and "quick" breads. (These breads—soda bread and cornbread, for example—which use a chemical leavening agent rather than yeast, consequently have a texture more like a cake or biscuit than a yeasted loaf.) However, over years of making cakes at Baker & Spice we have found that many are improved texturally by adding a little baking soda or baking powder with the self-rising flour. There is always a trade-off in such experiments, though—add too much and it will leave a bitter chemical taint in the mouth. The cake will also have a tough crumb.

Different brands of self-rising flour contain different amounts of leavening agent. The suggested additional leavening agent must therefore be treated as a guide and not an absolute.

Chocolate génoise royale

Génoise cakes are made by a French technique, which some people brought up making traditional American cakes initially find tricky. However, an electric mixer helps you achieve a consistent light result easily.

Génoise sponges are best baked the day before they are needed as they will slice better. In fact, they can be refrigerated for up to 3 days or, well wrapped in plastic wrap, can be frozen for 2 weeks without deteriorating. If ever a génoise comes out rather dry, prick the surface deeply with a needle all over and spoon on some rum or brandy, then leave for 12 hours before serving.

This very rich chocolate mousse génoise is based on a recipe developed by our first pastry chef, Henri Berthaux. It makes a fine dessert cake.

MAKES A 9-INCH CAKE

GÉNOISE
1/4 CUP (60 G) UNSALTED BUTTER
4 EGGS
HEAPED 1/2 CUP (115 G) SUPERFINE SUGAR
1 CUP (115 G) CAKE FLOUR
2/3 CUP (60 G) UNSWEETENED COCOA POWDER

CHOCOLATE MOUSSE
3/4 CUP (150 G) SUPERFINE SUGAR
3 EGGS, SEPARATED + 3 EGG YOLKS
1 TABLESPOON UNSWEETENED COCOA POWDER
SCANT 1 CUP (200 ML) HEAVY CREAM
1/2 CUP (100 G) UNSALTED BUTTER, DICED
8 OZ. (250 G) BITTERSWEET CHOCOLATE, CHOPPED
1 TABLESPOON BRANDY

DECORATION
3 OZ. (75 G) BITTERSWEET CHOCOLATE, CHOPPED
UNSWEETENED COCOA POWDER

Preheat the oven to 325°F. Butter a 9-inch springform cake pan. Line the bottom with a disk of parchment paper.

Make the génoise: melt the butter in a pan over a low heat. Remove immediately and let cool. Put the eggs and sugar into the bowl of a heavy-duty electric mixer fitted with the whisk and beat at a medium speed until the mixture rises. This will take 6–10 minutes. It is very important to incorporate as much air as possible at this stage to ensure a light result. Continue to beat until you achieve a ribbon consistency (1), when the mixture will be quite stiff and an off-white, cream color.

Remove the bowl from the mixer. Sift the flour and cocoa, and add to the bowl. Incorporate by stirring gently (2, 3). Pour in the melted butter and, using a rubber spatula, starting from the center at the base and working outward and upward, fold the mixture over while rotating the bowl a quarter turn (4). Repeat three more times, which means you will have turned the bowl one complete revolution after completing the fourth fold. This is the best way of mixing all the ingredients thoroughly without losing too much air by being heavy-handed—if you overwork the batter at this point you will end up with a flat and heavy cake.

Pour the batter into the cake pan, using the spatula to scrape the last of it from the mixing bowl. Put in the oven on the middle rack. Bake for 20 minutes.

Then, working quickly to keep heat loss to a minimum, open the oven door and test that the cake is done by inserting a skewer into the center. If the skewer comes out clean then the cake is ready. If sticky crumbs adhere to the skewer, give the cake another 5 minutes baking and test again. It may possibly still need another 5 minutes. When satisfied it is completely cooked, remove to a wire rack to cool before unmolding.

continued on page 98

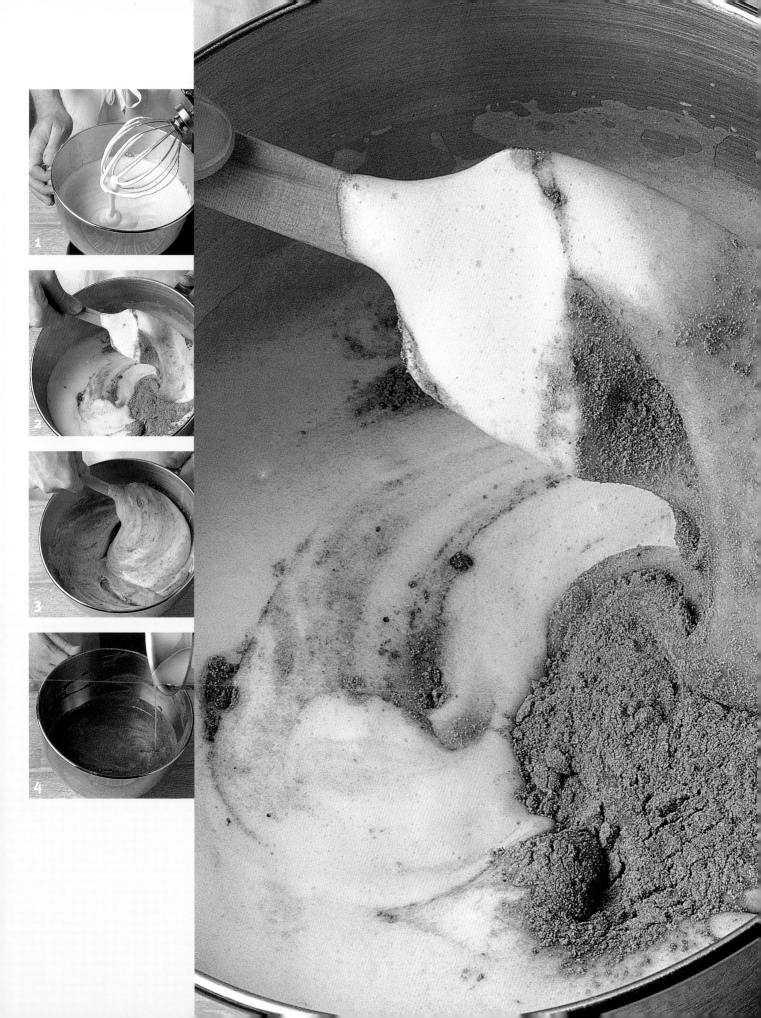

Carefully slice off the risen center of the cake to give a flat surface. Wash and dry the springform pan. Cut a strip of parchment paper to fit around the inside of the pan. Put the prepared génoise back in and reserve.

To make the chocolate mousse, put ¼ cup (50 g) of the sugar, the 6 egg yolks, cocoa powder, and cream in a bowl set over a pan of simmering water. Stir with a wooden spoon until the mixture is hot and thickens sufficiently to coat the back of the spoon. (If confident, you can make the custard in a saucepan over a low heat, which has the benefit of being much quicker.) Remove from the heat and gradually beat in the butter and chocolate until melted and fully combined. Stir in the brandy. Beat the egg whites with the remaining sugar to soft peaks, then fold them into the chocolate mixture.

Pour the mousse mixture on top of the génoise base in the pan. Cover and refrigerate for 4 hours or overnight before unmolding.

When ready to serve, unmold carefully by sliding a warm metal spatula around the inside of the pan before unclipping the side. Leave the cake on the pan base.

For the decoration, melt the chocolate in a bowl set over a pan of just simmering water. Pour onto a clean, dry metal cookie sheet and spread out thinly. As the chocolate cools, test it every so often—you want to catch it before it sets hard. When the chocolate is firm enough to work with, shave off large curls using a metal spatula. Transfer the curls carefully to the top of the cake, piling them up. Finish with a dusting of cocoa powder.

For a plain génoise, just omit the cocoa powder. A slice of plain génoise with seasonal berries or a fruit coulis makes a light and elegant dessert.

Chocolate pecan cake

The all-American pecan shares with walnuts a rich taste and a two-lobed appearance. Pecans also have a similar propensity for going rancid really fast, due to their high fat content, so they must be stored carefully—in a cool, dry place—and used up quickly. Don't freeze them, because when thawed they go odd very quickly.

The combination of chocolate and pecans in this cake is pleasing, not overly sweet like pecan pie so often is. The cake is very rich and buttery, however, and a small slice satisfies.

MAKES A 9-INCH CAKE

6 OZ. (180 G) BITTERSWEET CHOCOLATE, CHOPPED
$^3/_4$ CUP (180 G) UNSALTED BUTTER
4 EGGS, SEPARATED
$^3/_4$ CUP (140 G) SUPERFINE SUGAR
$2^1/_3$ CUPS (225 G) GROUND PECANS
$^2/_3$ CUP (100 G) ALL-PURPOSE FLOUR

ICING

12 OZ. (360 G) BITTERSWEET CHOCOLATE, CHOPPED
1 CUP + 2 TABLESPOONS (250 G) UNSALTED BUTTER
2 TABLESPOONS LIGHT CORN SYRUP

DECORATION

2 OZ. (50 G) WHITE CHOCOLATE, CHOPPED

Preheat the oven to 350°F. Butter a 9-inch springform cake pan. Line the bottom with a disk of parchment paper.

Make the cake: melt the chocolate and butter in a heavy-based pan over a low heat, then set aside to cool. Put the egg yolks and ½ cup (100 g) of the sugar in the bowl of a heavy-duty electric mixer fitted with the whisk, and beat until thick and light in color. In another bowl, beat the egg whites with the remaining sugar until they will hold a firm peak. Fold the melted chocolate into the whisked egg yolks, then fold in the ground pecans and flour. Finally, fold in the beaten egg whites.

Pour the cake batter into the pan. Bake in the center of the oven for 45 minutes to 1 hour or until a skewer inserted into the center of the cake comes out with a few slightly sticky crumbs clinging to it. Transfer to a wire rack and let cool completely in the pan.

To make the icing, combine the chocolate, butter, and corn syrup in a heavy-based pan, and warm over a low heat until smoothly combined. Remove from the heat and let cool to a thick, pouring consistency before using.

Remove the cake from the pan and place it on a rack set over a tray. Pour the icing over the cake, spreading it gently over the top and sides with a metal spatula.

For the decoration, melt the white chocolate in a bowl set over a pan of just simmering water. Put into a small parchment paper piping cone (or a small plastic bag), snip off the tip, and pipe in random lines over the chocolate icing on the top of the cake. Draw a skewer through the piped white icing to make squiggles or other decorative shapes. Let set before serving.

On cakes

"What makes a cake special are the quality of the ingredients, their generosity, and their freshness, not elaborate decoration. Our cakes are essentially simple constructions that are complete when they come from the oven. They are closer to good home baking than classic French pâtisserie, with its complex creams, additives, and custards. You don't have to have 20 stages to make something delicious.

"Small changes in the balance of ingredients can make big changes in the finished cake. There are no revolutions—things are made better very gradually, a natural process that takes time. This is the same as at home when a recipe is cooked over and over, with little changes and refinements each time." DORIT MAINZER, PASTRY COOK

Coffee layer cake with mascarpone cream

This recipe was given to us by David Whitehouse, who had a wonderful pâtisserie, Leamingtons of Richmond, which sadly closed some years ago. The pronounced coffee flavor in the cake provides the perfect balance for the rich mascarpone filling and frosting. Unusually for an English cake, the fat used is corn oil rather than butter.

MAKES AN 8-INCH CAKE WITH 2 LAYERS

$1^{1}/_{2}$ CUPS (225 G) SELF-RISING FLOUR
2 TEASPOONS BAKING POWDER
1 CUP + 2 TABLESPOONS (225 G) GRANULATED SUGAR
1 CUP (225 ML) CORN OIL
2 EGGS, SEPARATED
2 HEAPED TEASPOONS INSTANT COFFEE GRANULES DISSOLVED IN 2 TEASPOONS BOILING WATER
$^{1}/_{3}$ CUP (75 ML) WHOLE MILK

FROSTING AND FILLING
1 CUP (250 G) MASCARPONE
$^{1}/_{4}$ TEASPOON GRATED LEMON ZEST
3 CUPS (350 G) CONFECTIONERS' SUGAR, SIFTED
2 TABLESPOONS STRONG ESPRESSO, OR 2 HEAPED TEASPOONS INSTANT ESPRESSO DISSOLVED IN 2 TABLESPOONS BOILING WATER

Preheat the oven to 350°F. Butter two 8-inch springform cake pans and line the bottom of each with a disk of parchment paper.

Sift the flour, baking powder, and granulated sugar into a mixing bowl. Beat in the oil, egg yolks, coffee, and milk. In a second bowl, beat the egg whites to soft peaks. Stir a spoonful of the whites into the cake batter before gently folding in the rest. Divide the batter equally between the pans. Bake for about 45 minutes or until the cakes spring back when gently pressed in the center. Transfer to a rack to cool, unmolding the cakes while still warm and leaving them on the rack to cool completely.

For the mascarpone frosting, put the mascarpone and lemon zest in a bowl, and mix together with a spoon. Slowly add the confectioners' sugar, about one-third at a time, working each addition in completely with the spoon before adding the next, until you have a thick paste. Finally, beat in the coffee, a spoonful at a time, until it is completely incorporated.

Spread half the mascarpone cream on one cake layer, then put the second cake layer on top. Smooth the rest of the frosting over the top of the cake using a metal spatula.

Honey and spice cake

The very loose cake batter here delivers a light and airy result. Unusually, a little fresh ginger juice spikes the mixture, underpinning the more aromatic ground spices with its clean, hot taste.

MAKES 1 LARGE LOAF CAKE

$1^1/_2$-INCH PIECE GINGERROOT
$^1/_3$ CUP (125 G) CLEAR HONEY
$2^1/_2$ TABLESPOONS (50 G) LIGHT CORN SYRUP
10 TABLESPOONS (140 G) UNSALTED BUTTER
PACKED $^1/_4$ CUP (50 G) DARK BROWN SUGAR
2 EGGS
SCANT $^1/_2$ CUP (40 G) RYE FLOUR
$^2/_3$ CUP (100 G) SELF-RISING FLOUR
$^1/_2$ TEASPOON BAKING POWDER
$^1/_2$ TEASPOON GROUND CINNAMON
$^1/_2$ TEASPOON GROUND ALLSPICE

Peel the gingerroot, then grate onto a double thickness of cheesecloth. Holding the cheesecloth over a bowl, wind it around the ginger like a spring to squeeze out as much juice as you can. Discard the ginger pulp. Reserve the juice.

Preheat the oven to 325°F. Line the bottom and sides of a 2-pound loaf pan with parchment paper.

In a saucepan over a low heat, warm the honey, corn syrup, butter, and brown sugar until hot and the butter is almost melted. Transfer the mixture to the bowl of a heavy-duty electric mixer fitted with the whisk. Beat for $2^1/_2$ minutes at medium speed, then add the eggs and ginger juice, and continue beating for another $2^1/_2$ minutes. The mixture will have cooled, lightened with the air beaten into it, and thickened appreciably.

Sift together the flours, baking powder, and ground spices, then sift a second time. Fold the dry ingredients into the honey mixture using a spatula. The mixture will be unusually wet. Pour it into the pan and set on a baking sheet in the center of the oven. Bake for 50–60 minutes or until the top of the cake is a dark golden brown and it feels spongy, springing back lightly when gently pressed.

Transfer to a rack and let cool to room temperature in the pan before unmolding.

Marble cake

Swirling the chocolate through the batter gives the cake its distinctive appearance when cut and hence the name. This effect is best achieved by dividing the batter between two bowls, only adding the chocolate to one of them. The cake is then built with alternate spoonfuls.

MAKES 1 LARGE LOAF CAKE

4 OZ. (100 G) BITTERSWEET CHOCOLATE, CHOPPED
$^1/_2$ CUP (125 ML) MILK
$^1/_2$ CUP (120 G) UNSALTED BUTTER, SOFTENED
$^3/_4$ CUP + 2 TABLESPOONS (170 G) SUGAR
2 EGGS
$1^1/_2$ CUPS (225 G) SELF-RISING FLOUR
1 TEASPOON BAKING POWDER
$^1/_4$ CUP (65 G) SOUR CREAM

Preheat the oven to 325°F. Lightly grease a 2-pound loaf pan with melted butter. Cut a rectangle of parchment paper to fit the bottom of the pan and put it in place. Butter the paper, then dust the paper and the inside of the pan with a little flour.

Put the chocolate and 4 tablespoons of the milk in a bowl, and set over a pan of simmering water to melt. Remove from the heat.

In a heavy-duty electric mixer, cream the butter with the sugar until light in color and fluffy in texture. Slowly beat in the eggs, one at a time, until well combined. Sift the flour with the baking powder. Mix together the sour cream and remaining milk. Fold one-third of the flour into the butter and egg mixture, followed by a third of the sour cream mixture. Fold another third of the flour into the mixture, again with a third of the sour cream. Fold in the remaining flour and sour cream. Spoon half of the batter into another bowl. Add the chocolate mixture to one half and fold in.

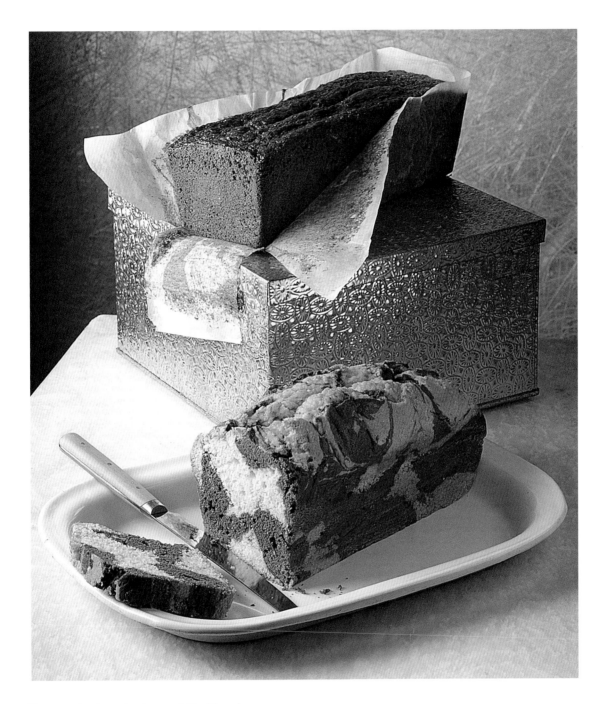

Honey and spice cake, top, and Marble cake

Spoon the two batters into the pan, taking it alternately from the bowls to give a marbled effect. Set the pan on a baking sheet in the middle of the oven and bake for 50–55 minutes or until a skewer inserted into the center of the cake comes out clean.

Let cool in the pan for 10 minutes, then run a knife between the cake and the sides of the pan. Very gently upturn the cake onto your cloth-covered hand, then place the cake upright on a wire rack to finish cooling.

Lemon cake

Lemon cake

Light yet full of flavor, this is a fresh-tasting cake with an appealing and strong lemon color.

MAKES 1 SMALL LOAF CAKE

3/4 CUP (115 G) SELF-RISING
FLOUR
1 TEASPOON BAKING POWDER
2 EGGS
HEAPED 1/2 CUP (115 G) SUGAR
1/4 CUP (65 ML) HEAVY CREAM
GRATED ZEST OF 1 LEMON
1 TABLESPOON LEMON JUICE
3 TABLESPOONS (45 G)
UNSALTED BUTTER, MELTED

ICING

1/4 CUP (30 G) CONFECTIONERS'
SUGAR
1 TEASPOON LEMON JUICE

Preheat the oven to 325°F. Lightly grease a 1-pound loaf pan with melted butter. Cut a rectangle of parchment paper to cover the bottom of the pan. Put the paper in place and butter it, then dust the paper and side of the pan with a little flour.

Sift together the flour and baking powder. Lightly beat the eggs with the sugar until just combined. Beat the cream into the eggs for a minute, then add the lemon zest and juice. Fold in the flour until lightly combined, then gently and carefully fold in the melted butter.

Pour the batter into the loaf pan. Set the pan on a baking sheet in the middle of the oven and bake for 45 minutes or until a skewer inserted in the center of the cake comes out clean. Let cool in the pan for 10 minutes, then run a knife between the cake and the sides of the pan. Very gently upturn the cake onto your cloth-covered hand, then place the cake upright on a wire rack to finish cooling.

To make the icing, sift the confectioners' sugar into a small bowl. Slowly add two-thirds of the lemon juice, stirring until combined. Add more lemon juice to make a thin icing, but be careful not to thin it too much—the icing will thin further when left for 2–3 minutes.

Brush the icing over the top of the cake, letting it drip a little down the sides.

Apricot cake

A rich batter produces a classic sponge cake, the apricots on the top nestling in the cake, which rises up around them as it bakes. Semi-ripe, firm plums can be used instead of apricots.

MAKES A 9-INCH CAKE

14 TABLESPOONS (200 G)
UNSALTED BUTTER,
SOFTENED
1 3/4 CUPS (350 G) SUGAR
3 EGGS
1 1/2 CUPS (225 G) SELF-RISING
FLOUR
2/3 CUP (150 G) SOUR CREAM
12 APRICOTS, CUT IN HALF AND
PIT REMOVED

TO FINISH

1/4 CUP (45 G) SUGAR

Preheat the oven to 325°F. Lightly grease a 9-inch springform cake pan with melted butter. Line the bottom with a disk of parchment paper and butter it, then dust the paper and the side of the pan with a little flour.

In a heavy-duty electric mixer, cream the butter with the sugar until light and fluffy. Slowly beat in the eggs, one at a time, until well combined. Fold one-third of the flour into the butter and egg mixture, followed by a third of the sour cream. Then fold in another third of the flour and sour cream. Finally, fold in the remaining flour and sour cream.

Spoon the batter into the prepared cake pan. Lay the fruit on the surface, cut-side up, leaning each apricot half slightly onto the next in concentric circles to cover the top completely. Finish by sprinkling with the extra sugar. Bake in the center of the oven for 50 minutes or until a skewer inserted into the center of the cake comes out clean.

Let cool in the pan for 10 minutes, then run a knife between the cake and the side of the pan. Release the clip on the side of the pan, lift off the collar, and leave the cake to cool completely on a rack.

Carrot cake

An American classic, carrot cake is unusual both in its use of a root vegetable in an otherwise very sweet construction and in using oil for the fat content rather than the more typical butter or margarine. The predominant flavor is of cinnamon, its potential stridency moderated by backnotes of nutmeg and cloves, the overall sweetness of the cake nicely balanced by the highly aromatic spicing. The cake's texture is made unusually moist by the carrots.

MAKES A 9-INCH CAKE WITH 2 LAYERS

2 CUPS (300 G) SELF-RISING FLOUR
1/4 TEASPOON BAKING POWDER
1/4 TEASPOON BAKING SODA
1 TEASPOON GROUND CINNAMON
1/2 TEASPOON GROUND CLOVES
1/4 TEASPOON GRATED NUTMEG
PINCH OF SALT
4 EGGS
1 1/2 CUPS (335 ML) SUNFLOWER OIL
2 1/4 CUPS (450 G) SUGAR
1 CUP (125 G) GRATED CARROTS
HEAPED 1 CUP (140 G) CHOPPED WALNUTS
2 TABLESPOONS HOT WATER

FROSTING

9 TABLESPOONS (130 G) UNSALTED BUTTER, SOFTENED
1 1/4 CUPS (300 G) CREAM CHEESE (PHILADELPHIA), SOFTENED
1 1/3 CUPS (160 G) CONFECTIONERS' SUGAR, SIFTED

Preheat the oven to 350°F. Lightly grease two 9-inch springform cake pans with melted butter. Line the bottom of each pan with a disk of parchment paper. Butter the paper, then dust the paper and the side of the pans with a little flour.

Sift together the flour, baking powder, baking soda, spices, and salt.

Separate 2 of the eggs.

In the bowl of a heavy-duty electric mixer, beat together the oil and the sugar. Slowly add the whole eggs, beating well, then beat in the 2 egg yolks. Beat in the grated carrots, then stir in the chopped walnuts. Fold in the sifted flour followed by the hot water. In another bowl, beat the 2 egg whites until soft peaks form. Fold them into the batter.

Divide the batter between the prepared pans. Set the pans on baking sheets in the middle of the oven and bake for 45 minutes to 1 hour or until a skewer inserted into the center of a cake comes out clean. Let cool in the pans for 10 minutes, then run a knife between the cakes and the sides of the pan. Release the clip, lift off the collar, and let the cakes cool on a rack.

To make the frosting, beat all the ingredients together to a thick cream. With a metal spatula, spread a layer of frosting on one cake, then press the other on top. Spread the rest of the frosting over the top and side of the cake, swirling it attractively. Refrigerate for at least 2 hours before serving, and keep in the fridge as the frosting will soften at room temperature.

Devil's food cake

Cakes bearing this rather provocative title, with all its implications of wicked excess, are often disappointing, typically being too sweet and not chocolatey enough. Our Devil's cake uses an unusually large amount of melted chocolate, to strike the right indulgent note.

MAKES A 9-INCH CAKE WITH 4 LAYERS

5 OZ. (150 G) BITTERSWEET CHOCOLATE, CHOPPED

HEAPED $^1/_2$ CUP (115 G) GRANULATED SUGAR

$^1/_2$ CUP (125 ML) MILK

SCANT $^1/_2$ CUP (40 G) UNSWEETENED COCOA POWDER

3 EGGS, SEPARATED + 1 EGG YOLK

$^2/_3$ CUP (150 G) UNSALTED BUTTER, SOFTENED

PACKED 7 TABLESPOONS (85 G) LIGHT BROWN SUGAR

$1^1/_2$ CUPS (225 G) ALL-PURPOSE FLOUR

1 TEASPOON SALT

1 TEASPOON BAKING SODA

$^3/_4$ CUP (170 G) SOUR CREAM

FROSTING

7 OZ. (200 G) BITTERSWEET CHOCOLATE, CHOPPED

$^2/_3$ CUP (60 G) UNSWEETENED COCOA POWDER

SCANT $^1/_2$ CUP (100 ML) WATER

1 TABLESPOON LIGHT CORN SYRUP

3 TABLESPOONS (45 G) UNSALTED BUTTER, SOFTENED

$2^1/_3$ CUPS (280 G) CONFECTIONERS' SUGAR

2 EGG YOLKS

Preheat the oven to 325°F. Butter two 9-inch springform cake pans and line the bottom of each with a disk of parchment paper.

Make the cake: put the chocolate, granulated sugar, milk, cocoa powder, and 2 egg yolks in a bowl set over simmering water. Stir to make a coherent custard-like mixture. Remove from the pan of water and reserve.

In the bowl of a heavy-duty electric mixer, beat the butter with the brown sugar until light and fluffy. Beat in the remaining 2 egg yolks, then the flour, salt, and baking soda. Fold in the sour cream followed by the chocolate mixture. In another bowl, beat the egg whites until they hold firm peaks, then fold gently into the cake mixture until combined.

Divide the batter between the pans and lightly smooth the top. Bake in the center of the oven for 45–50 minutes or until a skewer inserted into a cake comes out clean. Transfer to a rack and let cool completely in the pans.

To make the frosting, put the chocolate in a bowl and set over a pan of simmering water to melt. In a pan over a low heat, warm the cocoa powder, water, and corn syrup until hot but not boiling. Add the melted chocolate and whisk until combined. Remove from the heat and beat in the butter, confectioners' sugar, and egg yolks until smooth and creamy. Taste and add a little more sugar, if desired. Let cool until the frosting is thick but spreadable.

Remove the cakes from the pans and cut each into two layers. Put the four layers together, spreading a little frosting between them, and finish by frosting the top and side of the cake thickly, spreading the frosting with a metal spatula. Leave in a cool place overnight to firm, but not in the refrigerator, which would make the frosting dull.

Blueberry bran muffins

Eat these tender, moist muffins warm—they are never as nice when completely cold. Cranberries can replace the blueberries, if you prefer.

MAKES 18 MUFFINS

2 CUPS (100 G) BRAN
$1^1/4$ CUPS (300 ML) MILK
2 CUPS (300 G) SELF-RISING
FLOUR
2 TEASPOONS BAKING SODA
1 TEASPOON BAKING POWDER
3 EGGS
$^3/4$ CUP (160 G) GRANULATED
SUGAR
PACKED $^1/2$ CUP (85 G) LIGHT
BROWN SUGAR
$1^1/4$ CUPS (300 ML) SUNFLOWER
OIL
$1^1/4$ CUPS (200 G) BLUEBERRIES,
WASHED AND LEFT TO DRY

Preheat the oven to 325°F. Lightly oil a muffin pan or line with paper muffin cups.

Mix the bran and milk together. Set aside while you mix the other ingredients. Sift the flour, baking soda, and baking powder together. In a large bowl, lightly beat the eggs with the granulated and brown sugars and the oil. Fold in the sifted flour, then lightly fold in the soaked bran and milk. Finally, add the blueberries and fold lightly to combine. Do not overmix—there should still be some traces of flour evident.

Spoon the batter into the muffin cups to fill almost to the top. Bake in the center of the oven for 20–25 minutes. Let cool until warm, then eat immediately.

Chocolate hazelnut brownies

The moist interior of these brownies conjures up childhood memories of the joys of uncooked cake batters. For the right consistency, the batter should be mixed gently, not beaten hard.

MAKES 16 SQUARE BROWNIES

1/2 CUP (120 G) UNSALTED BUTTER, SOFTENED
1 1/4 CUPS (250 G) GRANULATED SUGAR
2 EGGS + 1 EGG YOLK
7 1/2 OZ. (210 G) BITTERSWEET CHOCOLATE, MELTED
1/4 CUP (60 ML) ESPRESSO
1 TABLESPOON RUM OR BRANDY
1 CUP + 2 TABLESPOONS (165 G) ALL-PURPOSE FLOUR
1 TEASPOON BAKING POWDER
1/4 TEASPOON SALT
WHOLE HAZELNUTS
CONFECTIONERS' SUGAR TO FINISH

Preheat the oven to 350°F. Cut a piece of foil to line the bottom and sides of a 9-inch square pan that is 2 inches deep.

Cream the butter with the granulated sugar. Slowly add the whole eggs, one at a time, and then the yolk, mixing well after each addition. Stir in the melted chocolate, then the coffee and the rum (or brandy). Sift the flour, baking powder, and salt together, and gently fold into the chocolate mixture.

Pour into the pan. Gently press some whole hazelnuts over the surface. Bake in the middle of the oven for 20–25 minutes: a skewer inserted near the center of the cake should come out warm at the tip and with slightly sticky crumbs clinging to it. (The greatest danger when baking brownies is overcooking, which turns them into dry chocolate cakes. It is therefore better to err on the side of underdone.)

Let cool in the pan before cutting into squares and dusting with confectioners' sugar.

Orange cheesecake brownies

A rippled effect is achieved by piping and swirling a sweet cheese mixture into the sticky chocolate batter. The contrast of flavor and texture is very appealing.

MAKES 16 SQUARE BROWNIES

1 1/2 CUPS (340 G) CREAM CHEESE, SOFTENED
1/2 CUP (100 G) SUGAR
1 EGG YOLK
SCANT 1/4 CUP (30 G) ALL-PURPOSE FLOUR
GRATED ZEST OF 1 ORANGE
1 TABLESPOON FRESHLY SQUEEZED ORANGE JUICE
1 RECIPE CHOCOLATE BROWNIES BATTER

Preheat the oven to 350°F. Cut a piece of foil to line the bottom and sides of a 9-inch square pan that is 2 inches deep.

Cream together the cream cheese and sugar. Add the egg yolk, followed by the flour. Finish by mixing in the orange zest and juice. It is important that the consistency be quite thick: achieving a similar texture to the chocolate brownie batter will make swirling the cheese mixture into the chocolate base easier. Put the cheese mixture into a pastry bag fitted with a 1/2-inch tip.

Spoon half of the brownie batter into the pan. Pipe half of the cheese over the top, moving from one side to another in swirling bands, pushing the cheese into the chocolate batter as you do so. Spoon on half of the remaining brownie batter, then pipe on the remaining cheese, pushing it into the chocolate as before. Finish by spooning on the last of the chocolate batter. Take a skewer and zigzag the swirls to accentuate the effect.

Bake as for Chocolate and hazelnut brownies, above.

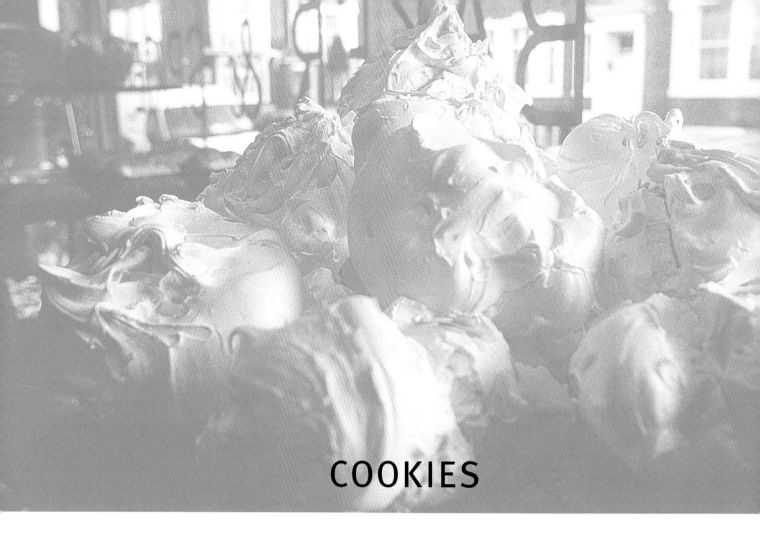

COOKIES

Cookies are delicious fripperies, never the main event perhaps, but nonetheless simple constructions which at their most delicate can please a discerning palate. In their sugary and more accessible forms they have given pleasure to children and the young-at-heart since medieval times, sweet mouthfuls that crunch appealingly and then burst with candied flavor on the tongue.

The term cookie describes a huge variety of sweet bites that range from thin disks or wafers, domed rounds, molded balls and crescents, and deep bars to fancy pressed and cut-out shapes. They may be lightly leavened—a small, flat cake can sometimes be a cookie (the word cookie, in fact, comes from the Dutch *koekje*, meaning "little cake")—and their texture can be soft and tender, chewy, or snapping-crisp. They may be tooth-achingly sweet with sugar or honey, or rich and buttery.

Chocolate cookies can be dry, with just a hint of chocolate, or moist, fudgy, and intensely chocolate-flavored. Dried fruit can outweigh the crumb in a recipe, but it does not stop the end result from being called a cookie. Meringues are cookies too, as are shortbread, ginger snaps, chocolate chip cookies, sugar-crusted langues-de-chat, biscotti, macaroons, and almond tuiles.

There are also savory bites, salty or flavored with cheese or anchovies, which are cookies in all but name. They are more likely to be called crackers, although their dough is much the same as a cookie dough and the baked texture like that of a cookie.

The first "cookies" were savory and not unlike the first breads, crude and coarse flat cakes bound with water and cooked on a griddle. Oat cakes were probably one of the first "cookies" ever made. With the wider availability of wheat, simple water and flour constructions became standard fare for travelers. Slow-baked twice to eliminate all moisture, this was the hardtack that sustained the early sailors, so hard it had to

be soaked in water before it could be chewed. It also had to be tough enough to resist infestation by insects, at least for several months—after a year at sea, the hardtack always seethed with weevils.

The first "sweet" cookies baked for culinary pleasure were served at the end of medieval banquets, and often contained sweetened fish and meats, along with the sugar and spices that proclaimed a person's wealth and generosity to the world. By the 1600s, sweet cookies were widely eaten in well-to-do households, typically little pieces of sweet pastry coated with sugar icing.

Cookies gradually developed national or cultural chracteristics, which are still identifiable today. Thin wafers perfumed with rose or orange-flower water and studded with slivered nuts are popular in the Middle East and North Africa, while American cookies still celebrate New World ingredients such as chocolate, pecans, and molasses. Cookies based on a stiff dough

that can be rolled out and cut into any shape often have attachments to religious festivals, some dating back to a pre-Christian era. One thinks of gingerbread men as well as the German Christmas *springerle*—glazed cookies in animal figures representing the Nativity, which are punched from a specially embossed rolling pin. In Britain, where sweet cookies and savory crackers are, confusingly, both called biscuits, the sweet variety often includes dried fruit and is invariably enjoyed with a cup of tea.

Shortbread

Shortbread is so-called because of its high fat content, short being the abbreviation of shortening, which in this rich, crumbly cookie means butter. At Baker & Spice we bake our shortbread in a rectangular pan, to be cut into bars, but if you prefer, bake it in traditional rounds.

MAKES 16 BARS OR 10–12 WEDGES

2/3 CUP (150 G) UNSALTED BUTTER
1 1/2 CUPS (225 G) ALL-PURPOSE FLOUR
1/4 CUP (30 G) CORNSTARCH
1/2 TEASPOON BAKING POWDER
1/4 TEASPOON SALT
3/4 CUP (150 G) SUGAR
1 TEASPOON VANILLA EXTRACT (OPTIONAL)

Lightly butter an 8 x 10-inch jellyroll pan (or two 6 1/2-inch fluted tart pans).

Dice the butter straight from the refrigerator and put into a mixing bowl to soften for about 30 minutes. Sift the flour, cornstarch, baking powder, and salt on top. Reserve 2 tablespoons of the sugar, and add the remainder to the bowl. (If using, add the vanilla too.) Rub the ingredients together gently between your fingertips and, as the mixture coheres, gather it gently into a ball. Alternatively, put the sifted flour, cornstarch, baking powder, salt, and sugar in the bowl of a heavy-duty electric mixer fitted with the whisk. Add the diced butter, then turn the machine on at low speed and mix until combined and the mixture resembles bread crumbs.

For bars, gently pack the mixture into the jellyroll pan. Incise the surface to mark out bars, cutting lengthwise in half and then across. Prick the top all over with a fork.

For a traditional presentation, shake some extra sugar onto a work surface, put the dough on it, and cut in half, shaping into two equal balls. Put each ball into a tart pan and gently press out into an even layer, making it slightly thicker at the edges and crimping between finger and thumb. Prick the surface all over with a fork and incise four bisecting shallow cuts from edge to edge like the spokes of a wheel, so that the round can be divided neatly into eight equal wedges when baked.

Refrigerate for 30 minutes to 1 hour. Toward the end of this time, preheat the oven to 350°F. Bake for 18–20 minutes or until the surface is slightly colored and the shortbread feels just firm to the touch. Let cool completely in the pans.

Benedict bar

Shortbread lends itself to a number of rich toppings. This one is similar to the South African Benedict cake. The idea came from Jeanne Hertz, who was a member of our talented pâtisserie team.

MAKES 16 BARS

7 TABLESPOONS (100 G) UNSALTED BUTTER
5 TABLESPOONS (60 G) SUGAR
1 TEASPOON VANILLA EXTRACT
2 CUPS (200 G) SLICED ALMONDS
3 TABLESPOONS MILK
1 RECIPE SHORTBREAD DOUGH
RASPBERRY JAM

Preheat the oven to 350°F. Lightly butter an 8 x 10-inch jellyroll pan.

Put the butter, sugar, vanilla, almonds, and milk in a small, heavy-based saucepan over the lowest heat, and warm until the butter has melted, stirring occasionally. Remove from the heat and let cool.

Press the shortbread dough into the pan. Spread a thin layer of jam over the surface, then spread the almond topping mixture over the jam. Bake as for Shortbread above, allowing 25–30 minutes.

Benedict bar

Date shortbread bars

Chewy, sweet, and aromatic, the date filling with its citrus tang of orange and smoky cinnamon contrasts nicely with the crisp and buttery cookie.

MAKES 16 BARS

8 OZ. (250 G) PITTED DATES
GRATED ZEST OF 1 ORANGE
2 TABLESPOONS (25 G)
UNSALTED BUTTER
1 TEASPOON GROUND CINNAMON
SCANT 1 CUP (200 ML) WATER
1 RECIPE SHORTBREAD DOUGH
(PAGE 116)

Preheat the oven to 350°F. Lightly butter an 8 x 10-inch jellyroll pan.

Put the dates, orange zest, butter, cinnamon, and water in a saucepan and bring to a boil. Remove from the heat and let cool before putting the mixture in a food processor. Pulse-chop to a coarse paste and use at once.

Press two-thirds of the shortbread dough into the pan. Spread the date mixture over the surface. Sprinkle the remaining shortbread dough on top like the topping for a fruit crisp. Bake for 25–30 minutes. Let cool in the pan.

Bitter chocolate cookies

With an exquisitely crisp exterior and a contrasting soft, chewy center, these elegant cookies crunch when bitten, then melt in the mouth. Use a bitter chocolate such as Valhrona Grand Caraque.

MAKES 20–30 COOKIES

$^3/_4$ CUP (110 G) ALL-PURPOSE
FLOUR
$^1/_3$ CUP (30 G) UNSWEETENED
COCOA POWDER
1 TEASPOON BAKING SODA
$^1/_2$ TEASPOON SALT
4 OZ. (115 G) BITTERSWEET
CHOCOLATE
2 OZ. (50 G) BITTER CHOCOLATE
$^1/_3$ CUP (80 G) UNSALTED BUTTER
PACKED $^3/_4$ CUP +
2 TABLESPOONS (175 G)
LIGHT BROWN SUGAR
1 EGG

Sift together the flour, cocoa powder, soda, and salt. Melt the chocolates together in a bowl set over a pan of simmering water, then let cool.

In a heavy-duty electric mixer, cream the butter with the sugar, beating at high speed until pale and creamy. Slowly add the egg and beat until combined. Fold in the sifted flour and cocoa mixture, then fold in the melted chocolate. Cover and let rest in the refrigerator for 1 hour.

Preheat the oven to 350°F.

Roll the dough into egg-sized pieces between your palms and place on buttered cookie sheets, leaving space for them to spread as they cook. Press them down slightly with your fingers to flatten. Bake for 15–20 minutes or until the edges are firm; the center should still give a little to the touch. Let cool on the sheets for a minute, then remove to a wire rack to cool completely.

Eat immediately or store in an airtight tin or cookie jar for up to 5 days.

Oatmeal and raisin cookies

Moist, sweet, and irresistible, these oatmeal and raisin cookies are enjoyed by adults and children alike. For a more sophisticated flavor, soak the raisins in brandy for a couple of hours before incorporating them into the dough.

MAKES 20 COOKIES

$^1/_2$ CUP (115 G) UNSALTED BUTTER,
SOFTENED
PACKED $^1/_2$ CUP (100 G) LIGHT
BROWN SUGAR
HEAPED $^1/_2$ CUP (115 G)
GRANULATED SUGAR
1 EGG, LIGHTLY BEATEN
$^1/_4$ CUP (60 ML) WATER
2 TEASPOONS VANILLA EXTRACT
$^2/_3$ CUP (100 G) SELF-RISING FLOUR
1 TEASPOON SALT
3 CUPS (250 G) ROLLED OATS
$^2/_3$ CUP (100 G) RAISINS

Preheat the oven to 350°F. Line two cookie sheets with parchment paper.

In a heavy-duty electric mixer, cream the butter with the sugars until light and fluffy. Gradually add the egg, beating until evenly combined. Then beat in the water and the vanilla before folding in the remaining ingredients.

Roll the dough into walnut-sized pieces between your palms and put them on the cookie sheets, leaving space between the cookies to allow for expansion as they cook. Bake for 15 minutes or until firm but still with some give to the gentle press of a finger. Let cool on the sheets for a few minutes before transferring to a wire rack.

Chocolate chip cookies

The chocolate chip cookie was created by accident and we know precisely when, where, and by whom. In 1933, Ruth Wakefield, who owned the Toll House Inn in Whitman, Massachusetts, added chocolate chips to a cookie dough, assuming they would melt and merge during baking to produce a uniformly textured chocolate-flavored wafer. Instead the pieces of chocolate stayed moistly intact, and the chocolate chip cookie was born.

The Baker & Spice version of this American institution is intensely flavored, rich, and chewy. They are appreciated by Baker & Spice's many U.S. expatriate customers, who say the cookies make them nostalgic for home. We use ready-made chocolate chips, but you can cut small pieces from a block of good-quality chocolate if you prefer.

MAKES ABOUT 30 COOKIES

^{3}/4 CUP (160 G) UNSALTED BUTTER, SOFTENED

PACKED 7 TABLESPOONS (85 G) LIGHT BROWN SUGAR

7 TABLESPOONS (85 G) GRANULATED SUGAR

2 EGGS

2^2/3 CUPS (400 G) ALL-PURPOSE FLOUR

^{1}/2 TEASPOON BAKING SODA

^{1}/2 TEASPOON BAKING POWDER

^{1}/4 TEASPOON SALT

HEAPED 1 CUP (200 G) SEMISWEET CHOCOLATE CHIPS

Preheat the oven to 350°F.

In the bowl of a heavy-duty electric mixer fitted with the whisk, cream the butter with the sugars until light and fluffy. Add the eggs, one at a time, waiting until the first is completely incorporated before adding the second, to avoid the mixture splitting. Sift together the flour, baking soda, baking powder, and salt, then fold into the mixture, followed by the chocolate chips, using a spatula. You will have a stiff dough.

Roll walnut-sized pieces of dough between your palms and put them on two buttered cookie sheets, leaving space between the cookies to allow for expansion as they cook. Bake for 15–20 minutes or until the edges are firm but the center still has some give to the gentle press of a finger.

Let cool on the sheets for a minute before transferring to a wire rack to cool to room temperature. Eat immediately or store in an airtight tin or cookie jar for up to 5 days.

(Opposite) Oatmeal and raisin cookies on plate and Chocolate chip cookies in glass jar

Pecan butter cookies

The butter really is the defining ingredient in these cookies, and its quality makes all the difference. Seek out a really good French butter, such as one from Normandy. It will make the cookies memorable.

MAKES ABOUT 30 COOKIES

1^1/$_3$ CUPS (300 G) UNSALTED BUTTER, SOFTENED
5 TABLESPOONS (60 G) GRANULATED SUGAR
1^1/$_4$ CUPS (140 G) COARSELY CHOPPED PECANS
2^1/$_3$ CUPS (350 G) ALL-PURPOSE FLOUR
PINCH OF SALT
CONFECTIONERS' SUGAR

Preheat the oven to 350°F. Line two cookie sheets with parchment paper.

Cream the butter with the sugar until light in color and texture. Beat in the pecans, then fold in the flour and salt.

Roll walnut-sized pieces of dough between your palms and put them on the cookie sheets, leaving space between the cookies to allow for expansion as they cook. Flatten them a little with your fingers. Bake for 15–20 minutes or until firm but still with some give to the gentle press of a finger. Let cool on the sheets for a few minutes before transferring to a wire rack. Toss in confectioners' sugar while still warm.

Lemon butter cookies

The pronounced lemon flavor balances the butter richness to perfection in these beautiful amber disks, which bake to a golden crisp at the rim.

MAKES 30–36 COOKIES

HEAPED ^{1}/$_2$ CUP (115 G) SUGAR
GRATED ZEST OF 2 LEMONS
^{1}/$_2$ CUP (115 G) UNSALTED BUTTER, CUT IN ^{3}/$_4$-INCH DICE
3 EGG WHITES
^{3}/$_4$ CUP (115 G) ALL-PURPOSE FLOUR
^{1}/$_2$ TEASPOON VANILLA EXTRACT
1 TABLESPOON LEMON JUICE
^{1}/$_4$ TEASPOON SALT

Blitz the sugar and lemon zest briefly in a food processor, processing until just combined, which should take about 30 seconds. Scrape down the sides and blitz for another 30 seconds. Scrape again, then add the butter and work until creamy—a few seconds. With the processor at full speed, add the egg whites through the feeder tube. Continuing to process, add the flour a spoonful at a time. When it is all incorporated, add the vanilla, lemon juice, and salt, and work to a thick batter-like dough. Transfer to a mixing bowl and beat for a minute with a wooden spoon. Cover the top with plastic wrap and let rest for 20 minutes.

Preheat the oven to 375°F. Butter two cookie sheets and dust lightly with flour. Drop heaped teaspoons of dough on the sheets, trying to place 15–18 equidistantly on each sheet and leaving the maximum amount of space between each blob to allow for spreading. Put both sheets in the center of the oven and bake for about 10 minutes or until the edges of the cookies start to brown. If you can't fit both sheets on the same shelf, bake in two batches.

Transfer the cookies to a wire rack with a spatula and let cool.

Pecan butter cookies

Almond tuiles

Tuiles are pliant when hot, so when you set them over a mold, they retain that shape when they firm during cooling. This makes them ideal as edible containers or to fill like brandy snaps. They are also delicious, brittle enough to snap on the first bite, exploding in the mouth with a pleasingly chewy finish, almost like caramel.

MAKES ABOUT 30 TUILES

1^1/3 CUPS (150 G) SLIVERED ALMONDS
^{3}/4 CUP (150 G) SUGAR
7 TABLESPOONS (60 G) ALL-PURPOSE FLOUR
1 EGG, SEPARATED + 1–2 EGG WHITES
3 TABLESPOONS (40 G) UNSALTED BUTTER, MELTED

Preheat the oven to 350°F. Line a cookie sheet with a nonstick baking liner or parchment paper.

In a bowl, mix together the almonds, sugar, and flour. Add the egg yolk, stirring it in, then 2 of the egg whites to form a stiff batter that should fall thickly off the spoon. If too thick, add the remaining egg white, a little at a time. Stir in the melted butter.

Spoon 2 teaspoons of the batter onto the cookie sheet and spread out into a 4-inch round using a fork dipped in cold water. Make another three rounds on the sheet, then bake for 5–10 minutes or until the edges of the cookies have turned brown.

Immediately lift the cookies off the sheet with a metal spatula and drape over a long, thin rolling pin. The cookies will harden almost at once into curved "tuiles" (roof-tile shapes), which you can then slide off. Alternatively, place the cookies over upturned tumblers, pulling down the edges gently to produce cups. Continue baking and shaping the cookies until all the batter is used up.

Parmesan disks

The ultimate, rich cheese cracker, made just like icebox cookies, these are the perfect accompaniment to any aperitif and go particularly well with dry sherry. You can substitute a well-flavored sharp Cheddar for the Parmesan if you prefer.

MAKES 40–50 CRACKERS

2¼ CUPS (335 G) ALL-PURPOSE
FLOUR
3 CUPS (300 G) FRESHLY
GRATED PARMESAN
1⅓ CUPS (300 G) UNSALTED
BUTTER, CHILLED
AND DICED
¼ TEASPOON CAYENNE PEPPER
1½ TEASPOONS SALT
1 TEASPOON COARSELY GROUND
BLACK PEPPER
1–2 TABLESPOONS WATER

TO FINISH

1 EGG, LIGHTLY BEATEN
2 TABLESPOONS SESAME SEEDS
2 TABLESPOONS BLACK ONION
SEEDS (NIGELLA)

Put the flour, freshly grated Parmesan, and chilled diced butter in a food processor with the cayenne, salt, and black pepper. Whiz to a crumb, then slowly add the cold water through the feeder tube until the dough forms into a ball.

Scrape out onto a lightly floured surface and roll into a cylinder. You will cut the disks from this, so size the roll accordingly. Wrap tightly in plastic wrap and refrigerate for at least 4 hours or overnight.

Brush the cylinder with beaten egg and roll in the mixed sesame and nigella seeds to coat all over. Wrap and chill for a further hour.

Preheat the oven to 350°F. Cut the cylinder into ¼-inch-thick slices and lay these on nonstick cookie sheets, leaving at least ³/₄-inch space around them. Bake for 20–25 minutes or until golden brown. Transfer to a wire rack to cool.

Meringues

Baker & Spice meringues are big—about 4 inches across. People eat them on their own, sweet, crisp, and as light as air.

Laurent Beauvois, who works in the shop, says they have always been a favorite with regular customers, particularly with children, whose eyes light up at the sheer scale of the treat. "They are always a great conversation piece in the shop," he says. "People are surprised by the size and the intensity of the whiteness. They are literally the first display you see when you step through the door."

The difference in texture between our meringues and others comes from warming the egg whites and sugar over hot water before prolonged whisking, during which the meringue cools as it stiffens. Putting the meringues into a preheated oven at a slightly higher temperature than is usual and then turning the heat off and leaving them overnight is a way of introducing consistency into the product.

The professional baker always uses egg whites by weight. This is much more accurate than counting them. For the weight here you will need 3–4 extra large eggs.

MAKES 12 MERINGUES

4 OZ. (115 G) EGG WHITES
1 CUP + 2 TABLESPOONS (225 G) SUPERFINE SUGAR
$^1/_3$ CUP (30 G) SLICED ALMONDS

Preheat the oven to 300°F. Cover two large cookie sheets with nonstick baking liners or parchment paper.

Put the egg whites and sugar in a bowl set over a pan of simmering water, and stir until the sugar has dissolved and the mixture is quite warm to the touch. Transfer the mixture to the metal bowl of a heavy-duty electric mixer and beat with the whisk attachment until thick and cool, about 15 minutes.

Spoon 6 large mounds of meringue onto each sheet. Lightly sprinkle with the almonds. Place the sheets in the oven, turn off the heat, and let the meringues dry out overnight.

Serve whole meringues with...

... a fruit coulis

... vanilla or chocolate ice cream

... whipped cream

... thick vanilla yogurt and seasonal berries

Or, toss berries with kirsch and sugar, mix with whipped cream and crushed meringues, and then freeze as a parfait. Or, ripple pieces of meringue through homemade ice cream by adding them in the last few minutes of churning.

Pastries

A form of thin sheet pastry rather like filo was known in Roman times, and basic pastry in the form of virtually inedible food containers for pies was a feature of medieval cooking. In ever more sophisticated variations, pastry has been an essential part of a developed Western kitchen since the fifteenth century. In the 1420s, an enterprising French cook incorporated butter into the folding and rolling process to create the first flaky pastry. Flaky remains to this day the finest example of the pastry cook's skill.

Today, pastry describes a multitude of different forms, from a basic short pastry for tart shells—the "short" referring to fat, as in the word shortening still used in America—through ever more buttery variations, to arrive at perfect puff pastry and, its ultimate and complex expression, the croissant. Pastry also includes hot-water crusts—robust lard-based constructions for stand-alone pies—and choux, the least pastry-like pastry, a pipeable soft paste made elastic with eggs.

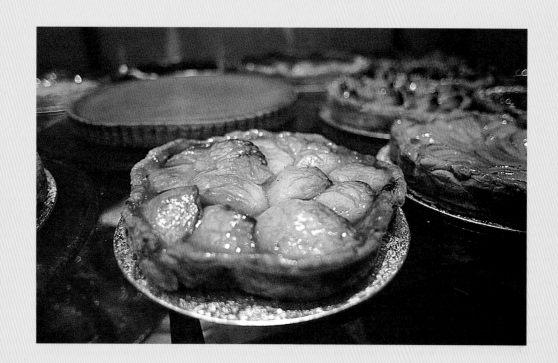

MAKING PASTRY

The kitchen is not a laboratory, but comes closest to a scientific environment when we make pastry, where precision is essential. With most cooking, we can make guesses based on experience. Pastry does not lend itself to such random modification, though everybody adapts and changes recipes. When these changes work, the minor adjustments they represent may be seen as incremental improvements, but do not look for revolutionary new methods. They do not exist. The first rule of pastrymaking is to have an accurate set of measures or scales and always to use them.

Pastry, particularly when cold butter is being added, does not react well to heat, which is why in restaurants and bakeries the pastrymaking is kept as far away from the ovens as possible. You, too, should always work in as cool an environment as is feasible. A marble sheet for pastrymaking is the perfect cold work surface, and this can be bought from kitchenware stores. It is desirable but certainly not essential.

Sweet pastry

This takes only seconds to make in a food processor, so it is a good idea to prepare two tart shells at the same time. One can be frozen, and then baked blind straight from the freezer without the necessity for a foil lining and weights, which means you can have a pastry shell almost instantly.

MAKES 2 TART SHELLS OF 10-INCH DIAMETER

3^1/$_3$ CUPS (500 G) ALL-PURPOSE FLOUR
^{3}/$_4$ CUP (150 G) SUGAR
1 CUP (100 G) GROUND ALMONDS
1^2/$_3$ CUPS (380 G) UNSALTED BUTTER,
    CHILLED AND DICED INTO SMALL CUBES
1 EGG + 2 EGG YOLKS
^{1}/$_2$ TEASPOON GRATED LEMON ZEST
1 TEASPOON RUM OR BRANDY
PINCH OF SALT

Put the flour, sugar, and almonds into a food processor and process at full speed for a few seconds. Add the butter dice and work again until just blended in. The mixture will resemble fine bread crumbs. Add the whole egg and yolks, the lemon zest, rum or brandy, and a minute pinch of salt, and work again briefly until the pastry balls.

Scrape out onto a sheet of plastic wrap and either shape into a rough ball or roll into a cylinder about 2 inches in diameter. Wrap and chill for at least 2 hours. Because of its high fat content, this pastry can be kept in the refrigerator for a week, and it freezes well.

The amount of butter makes it difficult to roll out this pastry dough, so it is best to do this between two sheets of parchment paper. Divide the dough in half. For each tart shell, roll out one portion to a round about 2 inches larger than the top of a 10-inch tart pan with a removable bottom.

Peel off the top sheet of parchment, then carefully pick the pastry up on the bottom sheet. Lay the pastry over the pan, paper-side up, and gently peel off the paper as you lift and ease the pastry down the sides of the pan to fit, taking care not to leave any air between the pastry and the pan. If the pastry has been rolled too thin, fold the overhanging pastry back over to give a double thickness around the edges. Squeeze this between finger and thumb to amalgamate, making sure that the top of the pastry is just above the height of the sides of the pan, as the pastry will shrink back during cooking.

Alternatively, cut thin disks from the cylinder of dough and arrange them, slightly overlapping, to cover the bottom and sides of the tart pan, pushing down to make a coherent shell. Take care to press into the corner where the sides and base meet so there is no air between the pan and the pastry. Make the edges slightly more solid than the base, and push the pastry slightly above the sides of the pan.

To bake "blind" (in other words unfilled), preheat the oven to 375°F. Line the pastry shell with a sheet of foil and fill with pie weights or dried beans. Bake for 15 minutes. Remove the foil and weights. Reduce the oven temperature to 300°F. Return the pastry shell to the oven to bake for another 15 minutes so the base can finish cooking to a uniform pale golden-brown.

Lemon tartlets

The pâtissier's version of lemon tartlets uses a lot of butter and is therefore extremely rich. It is an elegant dessert with a delicate but still lemony flavor.

MAKES 10 TARTLETS

1 RECIPE SWEET PASTRY
(PAGE 131)
8 EGGS
$^1/_4$ CUP (35 G) CORNSTARCH
GRATED ZEST AND JUICE OF
4 LEMONS
1 CUP + 3 TABLESPOONS
(235 G) SUGAR
1 CUP (225 G) UNSALTED
BUTTER, CUT INTO SMALL
DICE

DECORATION (OPTIONAL)
BITTERSWEET
CHOCOLATE, MELTED

Preheat the oven to 325°F.

Roll out the pastry (or cut out disks) and use to line ten 4-inch diameter fluted tartlet pans with removable bottoms. Prick the tartlet shells with a fork (there is no need for a foil lining and pie weights). Bake "blind" for 20 minutes or until set and pale golden brown. Set aside to cool.

Lightly whisk together the eggs and cornstarch in a bowl.

Put the lemon zest and juice and the sugar in a large, heavy-based saucepan and bring to a boil. Remove the pan from the heat. Whisk a little of the lemon-sugar mixture into the eggs, then whisk this mixture back into the remaining lemon mix in the pan. Return the pan to a medium-low heat and bring to a simmer. Cook for 1 minute, whisking constantly, then remove from the heat. Add the butter a few pieces at a time, whisking quickly after each addition. Transfer to a wide container. Cover the surface with plastic wrap and let cool.

Put the lemon filling into a pastry bag fitted with a $^5/_8$-inch plain tip. Pipe into the baked tartlet shells, swirling it up into a peak. If you like, decorate with a swirled drizzle of melted chocolate.

Lemon curd tart

Lemon curd makes a very good tart filling and has the benefit of being pretty much foolproof in its preparation. The finish is quite sharp and those with a sweet tooth may want to add a further $^1/_4$ cup (50 g) sugar to the curd mixture. Lemons tend to be wax-coated and, unless organic, will have been chemically treated, so always scrub them in soapy water, then rinse and dry before using.

MAKES A 10-INCH TART

8 EGGS
$^1/_4$ CUP (60 G) UNSALTED
BUTTER
GRATED ZEST AND JUICE OF
6 LEMONS
1 CUP + 2 TABLESPOONS
(225 G) SUGAR
10-INCH SWEET PASTRY TART
SHELL (PAGE 131),
BAKED "BLIND"

Whisk the eggs together in a bowl. In a heavy-based saucepan, melt the butter over a low heat. Add the eggs, lemon zest and juice, and the sugar. Cook gently, stirring from time to time. When the mixture starts to thicken, stir constantly until a thick curd custard is formed.

Pour and spoon into the baked tart shell, and let cool and set before serving.

Lemon tartlets

Chocolate tart

Rich and dark, this tart is best eaten when the filling is warm but not hot. The better the chocolate, the better the tart. If desired, dust with confectioners' sugar and serve with whipped cream.

MAKES A 10-INCH TART

8 oz. (220 g) BITTERSWEET
CHOCOLATE, CHOPPED
$3/4$ CUP (180 g) UNSALTED
BUTTER
6 EGGS
$1^1/2$ CUPS (280 g) SUGAR
$1/2$ CUP + 1 TABLESPOON (85 g)
ALL-PURPOSE FLOUR
10-INCH SWEET PASTRY TART
SHELL (PAGE 131),
BAKED "BLIND"

Put the chocolate into a bowl set over a pan of simmering water. The base of the bowl should not touch the water. Stir from time to time with a metal spoon until the chocolate has melted into a coherent mass.

Preheat the oven to 350°F.

Put the butter, eggs, sugar, and flour into the bowl of a heavy-duty electric mixer fitted with the whisk. Switch on at medium speed. Pour in the melted chocolate and beat for 10 minutes.

Put the baked tart shell on a baking sheet and fill with the chocolate mixture. Bake for 20 minutes. Transfer to a wire rack and let cool until warm before serving.

Chocolate and caramel tart

The flavors of chocolate and caramel contrast perfectly, balancing bitterness and sweetness on the tongue. The combination is rich and satisfying, nicely offset by the crisp crunch of the short pastry. The tart filling also makes the ultimate topping for shortbread bars (page 116): pour the caramel mixture over the baked shortbread in its pan and let cool and set. Finish with the chocolate topping, then refrigerate before cutting into neat bars.

MAKES A 10-INCH TART

1 CUP + 2 TABLESPOONS
(225 g) SUGAR
SCANT $1/2$ CUP (100 ML) WATER
$2/3$ CUP (150 ML) LIGHT CREAM
$1/2$ CUP (115 g) UNSALTED
BUTTER, CUT INTO DICE
10-INCH SWEET PASTRY TART
SHELL (PAGE 131),
BAKED "BLIND"

CHOCOLATE TOPPING

6 oz. (170 g) BITTERSWEET
CHOCOLATE, CHOPPED
2 TABLESPOONS (30 g)
UNSALTED BUTTER

Put the sugar and water in a heavy-based saucepan and bring to a boil. Lower the heat and use a thermometer to take the caramel to 350°F, when it will be a deep golden-brown. Remove the pan from the heat and gradually add the cream—start with a spoonful at a time, because the mixture will foam up when the cold cream hits the incandescent caramel. When all the cream has been incorporated, gradually stir in the butter to give a smooth, creamy sauce. Pour into the baked tart shell and let set.

Put the chocolate in a bowl set over a pan of simmering water. When melted, remove from the heat and beat in the butter. Spread over the set caramel using a plastic spatula, then swirl the surface attractively with a skewer. Let cool completely before serving.

Chocolate and caramel tart

Butter puff pastry

Puff is the ultimate pastry, a really rich, multi-layered, and extravagantly buttery construction. Correctly made, it is so light one is not aware of its weight in the hand or its high fat content on the tongue. This is the supreme product of the pastry cook's alchemy: flaky, with each layer as thin, crisp, and fragile as the next, the whole made extraordinary by the air that separates them.

The skill in making puff pastry is to interleave the butter and air into the flour as it forms a dough by rolling, turning, and chilling, but while doing so to be as economical in the working as possible, to prevent over-working of the gluten in the flour. The consequence of too much rolling and stretching is elasticity. That is what you want in a bread dough, but in pastry it results in it shrinking back unacceptably. The chilling is also vital. If the butter softens it will become oily and seep through the flour, giving a greasy surface to the pastry layers and causing them to stick together, so inhibiting the rise.

Making puff pastry is not easy, although perhaps more time consuming than really difficult. But, of course, like anything technique-based, it gets better with repetition. It is best prepared a day ahead. The Baker & Spice technique of making a beurre manié, or kneaded butter, of flour and butter is different from most recipes, which interleave chilled butter into the pastry. It produces an excellent, buttery, flaky puff.

5

BUTTER PASTE

1 1/2 cups (340 g) unsalted butter, softened

1 cup (150 g) all-purpose flour

ASSEMBLY

3 3/4 cups (560 g) all-purpose flour + extra for sprinkling

4 egg yolks

3/4 cup (180 ml) water

2 teaspoons salt

Make the butter paste: put the butter and flour in the bowl of a heavy-duty electric mixer fitted with the paddle. Mix on the slowest speed until combined. Remove to a sheet of plastic wrap and shape into a rectangle about 1/4 inch thick. Wrap in the plastic and keep in a cool place (not in the refrigerator) while you make the dough.

For the assembly, put the flour, egg yolks, water, and salt in a bowl and mix to a dough. If necessary, add another teaspoon or two of water, but be careful—the dough will soften on resting. What you want is a smooth but fairly tight dough. Remove it to a lightly floured surface and knead for 10 minutes or until very smooth and elastic. Shape into a ball, wrap in plastic wrap, and let rest for 1 hour or, ideally, overnight.

Lightly flour the work surface and roll out the dough into a rough square about 3/8 inch thick. Place the rectangle of butter paste in the center and fold the corners of the dough over the top to cover the paste completely (1, 2). Wrap in plastic wrap and refrigerate for 30 minutes.

Place the dough on the lightly floured surface. Roll out, rolling away from you, into a long rectangle 14–16 x 26–28 inches and 1/2 inch thick (3, 4). Fold one short end in by a sixth and then the other short end in by a sixth (5). Fold both ends over again by a sixth so that they meet in the center (6). Now fold the two together, as if you are closing a book (7).

Next, turn the dough so the fold is to one side. Roll it out gently away from you again into a long rectangle about the same dimensions as before. Fold one short end of the dough in by a third (8) and then the other short end in by a third, over the top of the first third. This is a single "turn."

Spread a sheet of plastic wrap over a tray, place the dough on top, and cover tightly with plastic wrap. Let rest in the refrigerator or a cool place for 1 hour.

Set the dough on the floured work surface so the fold is to one side. Roll out into a rectangle again and give it a single turn, followed immediately by another single turn. Wrap in plastic wrap and leave in the refrigerator overnight before using.

On pastry

"Good ingredients are the foundation for excellent pastry. Take the finest you can find—the butter from your table, good dark chocolate, the cream you would serve with the sweetest strawberries—and search for the right flour, soft and unbleached. Never, ever economize on flour (one of the least expensive ingredients you will use), as its quality will enhance the flavor of everything you mix with it. Try to work in the morning, when the kitchen is cooler, and be methodical, measuring and mixing with a swift and careful hand.

"Pastrymaking is a skill that really does improve with repetition. You learn about getting it perfect by doing it over and over. Enjoy your work. Allow it to become a pleasure, and it will soon feel effortless. Remember that the best pastry is defined by the indulgence it encourages." DAN LEPARD, BAKER

Cheese straws

Traditional cheese straws are dense and very rich. Good-quality puff pastry provides an effortless opportunity to create a much lighter variation on the theme. These are delicious, yet quick and easy to make.

Include different spices with the cheese, giving a prickle of heat with chili flakes or taking this one step further by scattering on finely shredded fresh hot chilies. Add paprika for a smoky contrast, or shredded scallions or shallots to cut the richness of the cheese. Alternatively, Dijon mustard could be spread thinly on the pastry before adding the cheese. For a different effect, instead of sprinkling sesame seeds on top, substitute onion seeds or cumin seeds.

MAKES 20–25 STRAWS

14 OZ. (400 G) BUTTER PUFF PASTRY (PAGE 136)
SCANT 1 CUP (85 G) FRESHLY GRATED PARMESAN OR SHARP CHEDDAR
BLACK PEPPER
1 TABLESPOON SESAME SEEDS (OPTIONAL)

GLAZE
1 EGG YOLK
1 TABLESPOON MILK

Preheat the oven to 350°F. Line two cookie sheets with parchment paper.

Roll out the pastry into a neat rectangle about ¼ inch thick. Distribute the grated cheese evenly on half the pastry and grind black pepper over all. Fold the other half of the pastry over, pressing down gently. Cut across into ¼-inch-wide strips, then, holding the ends, twist each strip to make a spiral shape.

Beat the egg yolk and milk together in a bowl. Brush the cheese straws with this glaze and shake the sesame seeds over, if using. Lay the cheese straws on the cookie sheets.

Bake for 20–25 minutes or until puffed and golden brown. Remove to a rack and let cool before serving.

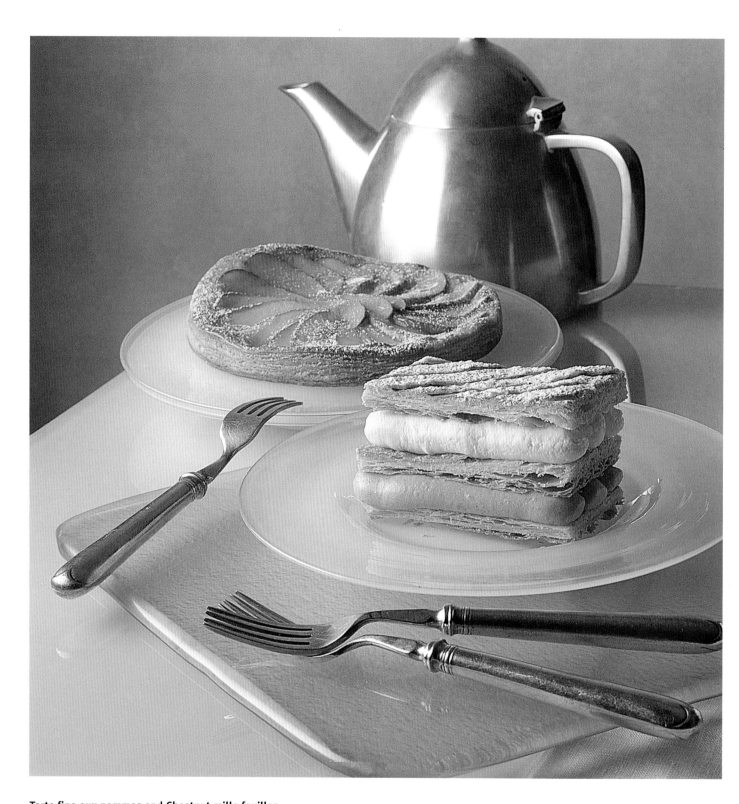

Tarte fine aux pommes and Chestnut mille feuilles

Chestnut mille feuilles

Mille feuilles—literally "thousand leaves"—is nothing more than slices of baked puff pastry layered in a triple-decker sandwich with a filling such as whipped cream and fruit or, as here, a rich chestnut cream. The success of everything you do with puff pastry is determined by its quality. You could make a pretty mille feuilles with bought puff pastry, but if this uses oil or a commercial solid margarine rather than butter, you would not want to eat it. Butter puff is essential.

It is suggested that you weight the pastry during baking with a wire rack, if you have one that will fit in the oven. This compensates for any unevenness in the rolling, which can result in an uneven rise. The rack does not stop the pastry from rising, but it does ensure a flat surface. It is not, however, essential.

SERVES 8

14 OZ. (400 G) BUTTER PUFF PASTRY (PAGE 136)
1 CUP (150 G) BOTTLED CHESTNUTS IN SYRUP, DRAINED
2 TABLESPOONS SIFTED CONFECTIONERS' SUGAR + EXTRA FOR DUSTING
1 VANILLA BEAN
1^1/$_4$ CUPS (300 ML) HEAVY CREAM

PASTRY CREAM
^{1}/$_4$ CUP (50 G) SUGAR
2 EGG YOLKS
3 TABLESPOONS (25 G) CORNSTARCH
1 VANILLA BEAN
1 CUP (250 ML) MILK
2 TABLESPOONS (25 G) UNSALTED BUTTER

First make the pastry cream. Whisk the sugar, egg yolks, and cornstarch together in a bowl. Split open the vanilla bean over a plate and scrape out the seeds. Put both the bean and seeds into a heavy-based saucepan with the milk and slowly bring to a boil. Remove from the heat and whisk a third of the hot milk into the egg mix. Quickly tip the egg mix into the milk pan, scraping any remaining egg from the sides of the bowl, and immediately whisk together. Return the pan to the heat and bring back to a boil, stirring constantly. Boil for 1 minute. Strain through a sieve into a bowl, discarding the vanilla seeds in the sieve (wash and dry the bean for making vanilla sugar). Add the butter and stir until melted. When the pastry cream has cooled to warm, cover the surface with plastic wrap and let cool completely.

Preheat the oven to 350°F. Line a baking sheet with a nonstick baking liner or parchment paper.

Roll out the puff pastry on a flour-dusted surface to a 12-inch square about ¼ inch thick. Lay the pastry square on the baking sheet. Put a wire rack on top of the pastry. Bake for 25–30 minutes or until the pastry is crisp and brown. Carefully turn the baking sheet over so that the pastry rests on the wire rack, then let cool in a warm, dry place.

Put the drained chestnuts in a food processor and pulse-chop briefly to a rough paste. Add 1¼ cups (300 ml) of the pastry cream (any left over can be used as a tart or éclair filling, or topped with fruit for a simple dessert). Sweeten with about 1 tablespoon of confectioners' sugar, or to taste. Split the vanilla bean and scrape the seeds into the mixture. Fold together, then cover and chill for 20–30 minutes.

Lightly whip the cream with the remaining tablespoon of confectioners' sugar to soft peaks. Fold one-third of the cream into the chestnut mixture.

Carefully transfer the pastry square to a work surface. Trim the edges with a sharp knife, then cut into three equal strips. (Alternatively, if you prefer to make individual mille feuilles, or napoleons, cut the pastry into 24 even-sized rectangles.)

Spread one strip of pastry with the chestnut custard, then lay a second strip on top. Spread the remaining whipped cream over this and finish with the final layer of pastry. With a metal spatula, remove any excess filling from the pastry, and dust the top of the mille feuilles with confectioners' sugar. For a decorative finish, score lines in the sugar with a hot skewer.

Pithiviers

The pithiviers is a classic of French pâtisserie. Make and bake it ahead of time—though it isn't complicated, you need to give yourself time and space to work in a cool kitchen, when the house is quiet and you can concentrate on perfecting the finish.

SERVES 8–10

1 LB. 2 OZ. (500 G) BUTTER
PUFF PASTRY
(PAGE 136)

ALMOND CREAM
2$^1/_2$ CUPS (250 G) GROUND
ALMONDS
1$^1/_4$ CUPS (250 G) SUGAR
1 CUP + 2 TABLESPOONS
(250 G) UNSALTED BUTTER,
SOFTENED
2 EGGS
$^1/_3$ CUP (50 G) ALL-PURPOSE
FLOUR

GLAZE
2 EGG YOLKS
1 TABLESPOON MILK

Make the almond cream: place the almonds, sugar, and butter in a food processor, and blend until smooth and the butter is thoroughly incorporated. Add the eggs and flour, and blend again for a moment to combine. Transfer the mixture to an 8-inch springform cake pan lined with plastic wrap and spread evenly. Cover and chill until firm.

Divide the puff pastry into two pieces, two-thirds and one-third. Roll out the smaller piece of dough into a rough round about 10 inches in diameter and $^1/_4$ inch thick. Place on a baking sheet lined with a nonstick baking liner or parchment paper.

For the glaze, lightly beat the egg yolks with the milk.

Take the almond cream out of the refrigerator and unmold from the pan. Center it on the round of pastry. Brush around the exposed pastry edge with the egg-yolk wash. Roll out the remaining larger piece of pastry to a round $^1/_4$ inch thick, and lay it carefully over the almond filling. Starting at the center, press and smooth out the pastry, sealing it close to the almond cream and the base round of pastry. Be careful not to trap any air bubbles underneath the pastry. If you do, lightly prick them with a pin. Now seal around the edges with a fork, pressing firmly down to seal the two rounds of pastry together.

Take a round bowl or dish that will enclose the filled part of the shaped pastry snugly inside. Press the bowl firmly down over the top so that the edge of the bowl indents lightly into the pastry edge. Remove the bowl, then cover the pithiviers with plastic wrap and refrigerate for 1 hour.

Brush the surface of the pithiviers with the egg-yolk wash. Let dry for 5–10 minutes. Now take a small, sharp knife and trim around the edge of the pastry, leaving a 1$^1/_4$-inch border. Cut a scalloped edge on the border, if desired. Very lightly score through the domed top of the pastry, drawing curved lines that radiate out from the center to the bottom of the dome. Finally, cut a small hole in the center of the dome, so that any air created as the pithiviers bakes will be released. Refrigerate, uncovered, until the oven is at temperature.

Preheat the oven to 350°F.

Remove the pithiviers from the refrigerator and bake for 15 minutes, then reduce the oven temperature to 300°F and continue to bake for 35–40 minutes or until risen and golden brown, and a skewer inserted through the hole in the center comes out clean. Carefully transfer the cooked pastry to a wire rack and let cool.

Serve warm with lightly whipped cream.

Plum tart

Plum tart

To be exceptional this tart is wholly dependent on the quality of the pastry used. Those who choose not to attempt to make their own puff pastry are in good company, and good frozen butter puff pastry can be substituted. Frangipane is the pretty French word for a rich nut confection.

MAKES A 10-INCH TART

12 SLIGHTLY UNDER-RIPE PLUMS
8 OZ. (225 G) BUTTER PUFF
PASTRY (PAGE 136)
$^1/_4$ CUP (80 G) APRICOT JAM

HAZELNUT FRANGIPANE
14 TABLESPOONS (200 G)
UNSALTED BUTTER
$^3/_4$ CUP (150 G) SUGAR
$1^1/_4$ CUPS (125 G) GROUND
ALMONDS
$1^1/_4$ CUPS (125 G) GROUND
HAZELNUTS
$^2/_3$ CUP (100 G) ALL-PURPOSE
FLOUR
3 EGGS

Make the frangipane: in the bowl of a heavy-duty electric mixer fitted with the whisk, beat the butter with the sugar at high speed until light and fluffy, about 8 minutes. Add the ground nuts and flour, and beat briefly. Add the eggs, one at a time, whisking to combine. Reserve.

Cut the plums in half, discarding the pits, then cut each half in half and reserve.

Preheat the oven to 375°F. Butter a 10-inch tart pan with a removable bottom.

Roll out the pastry dough into a thin round. Using the rolling pin, transfer the pastry into the pan and press in gently to line the bottom and sides. Fold the edges over to give thicker sides to the pastry shell, then roll gently but firmly over the top of the pan with the rolling pin to cut through the pastry and give a neat rim.

Spread the hazelnut frangipane in the pastry shell, then push the plum quarters into the frangipane so that they stand upright—that is, cut faces vertical. Bake for 15 minutes, then reduce the oven temperature to 300°F. Bake for a further 35–40 minutes, when the frangipane will have risen up around the plums and set. Remove from the oven to a rack and let cool a little before lifting the tart out of the pan.

Warm the jam in a small pan until melted. Press it through a sieve to remove any large pieces of fruit, then brush over the warm tart to glaze.

Tarte fine aux pommes

This is an absolutely classic French tartlet. We dust the apples with a spoonful of sugar just before the tartlets go into the oven and then add more gloss with a jam glaze after baking.

MAKES 4 TARTLETS

14 OZ. (400 G) BUTTER PUFF
PASTRY (PAGE 136)
4 TABLESPOONS PASTRY CREAM
(SEE CHESTNUT MILLE
FEUILLES, PAGE 141)
4 GRANNY SMITH APPLES
1 TABLESPOON SUGAR
2 TABLESPOONS APRICOT JAM

GLAZE
1 EGG YOLK
1 TABLESPOON MILK

Preheat the oven to 400°F. Line a baking sheet with a nonstick baking liner or parchment paper. Divide the pastry into four and roll out each portion into a thin round about 6 inches in diameter. Place on the baking sheet. Scrape the pastry cream over the pastry with a metal spatula to coat thinly.

Cut the apples into quarters and remove the cores, but leave the skins on. Slice the quarters in paper-thin slices and fan these on the pastry disks, with each new slice slightly overlapping the last. Leave a $^3/_8$-inch rim of pastry uncovered. Lightly beat the egg yolk with the milk, and brush this glaze over the pastry rim. Sprinkle the apples with the sugar.

Bake for 15 minutes, then lower the oven temperature to 300°F and bake for a further 5 minutes. The apples will have taken on a golden glaze while the pastry will have puffed up around the rim. Warm the jam in a small pan until melted. Press it through a sieve to remove any large pieces of fruit, then brush over the warm tartlets.

Pear tarte renversée

For a tarte Tatin, peeled and segmented apples are baked in caramel with a pastry lid on top; this becomes the base when the cooked tart is inverted for serving. When such a tart is made with any other fruit, such as the pears here, it should properly be called a *tarte renversée*, which means upside-down tart. The buttery caramel and fruit juices soak into the pastry when the tart is turned upside-down, so it should be served warm to be at its best, though not straight from the oven when people could burn themselves with the super-heated caramel.

Cooks develop their own little tricks to ensure a perfect result. At Baker & Spice we make the caramel first, then pour it into the mold and let it cool. The pears cook slowly as the caramel melts and mixes with the fruit juices, making it less likely that the caramel will burn. Use pears that are just ripe but still firm.

MAKES A 9-INCH TART

7–8 COMICE PEARS
JUICE OF ¹/₂ LEMON
1 LB. 2 OZ. (500 G) BUTTER
PUFF PASTRY (PAGE 136)

CARAMEL
1¹/₄ CUPS (250 G) SUGAR
²/₃ CUP (150 G) UNSALTED
BUTTER
SCANT ¹/₄ CUP (50 ML) WATER

Make the caramel: in a saucepan over a medium-low heat, warm the sugar, butter, and water, stirring to dissolve the sugar, then bring to a boil. Reduce the heat and cook until you have a dark caramel, on the reddish side of brown. Carefully pour the caramel into a 9-inch cake pan and tilt to cover the bottom evenly. Let cool while you prepare the fruit.

Preheat the oven to 375°F.

Peel the pears, cut in half, and remove the core. Put the halves in a bowl and toss with the lemon juice to prevent discoloration.

Roll out the pastry to about the thickness of a silver dollar. Using a plate 11–12 inches in diameter as a guide, cut out a round. Fold the round of pastry in half and then fold again to make a triangular shape. Arrange the pear halves in the pan, cut-side up, packing them closely together in a fan shape and filling all gaps. Lay the folded pastry over one-fourth of the pan and unfold to cover the fruit, tucking the edges of the pastry inside the rim of the pan.

Bake for 35–40 minutes or until the pastry is well risen and golden brown. Remove from the oven to a wire rack and let cool for 5–10 minutes.

Cover the top of the pan with a large flat plate, leaving a small gap at one side. Tilt to pour off any excess caramelly juices into a bowl; reserve these. Then, holding the plate and pan firmly together, invert the two. Sit the plate on a flat surface and lift the pan away from the tart. Cut in wedges and serve warm with whipped cream and the reserved caramelly juices.

Croissants

For 200 years, croissants, which originated in Vienna in the familiar crescent shape, were made from enriched bread dough. The delightfully buttery yet feather-light puff pastry and yeast croissant, which has become the definitive statement of a pastry cook's skill, is a comparatively recent French development, occurring perhaps 100 years ago. Making croissants is time-consuming and takes practice to get right, but since it is now difficult to buy a fine croissant, even in France, there is every reason to try. This is a much simpler method than most, yet it produces an excellent, flaky result.

Croissants are at their best when still warm from the oven. Their high butter content means that they freeze well and will not start to deteriorate in the freezer for at least 2 weeks. Before eating, they should be put frozen into a 500°F oven for 5 minutes, then removed to a rack and left to stand for 5 minutes. Unbaked, unrisen croissants also freeze well, as does any uncooked pastry. Raw croissants should be thawed in the refrigerator overnight, then left to rise, covered, until doubled in size before baking.

MAKES 16 CROISSANTS

1 PACKAGE QUICK-RISING ACTIVE
DRY YEAST
4 CUPS (500 G) WHITE BREAD
FLOUR + EXTRA FOR
SPRINKLING
$^1/_2$ CUP (110 ML) WARM
BOTTLED SPRING WATER
(68°F)
$^1/_2$ CUP (110 ML) COLD MILK
(50°F)
5 TEASPOONS SALT
$^1/_3$ CUP (70 G) SUGAR
1 CUP + 2 TABLESPOONS
(250 G) UNSALTED
BUTTER

GLAZE
1 EGG YOLK
1 TABLESPOON MILK

Make a sponge: in a bowl, whisk together the yeast, $^3/_4$ cup (100 g) of the flour, and the warm water. Cover the bowl with plastic wrap and leave in a warm place for 2 hours or until the sponge has risen by at least one-third and is clearly active, with lots of bubbles.

Put the remaining flour, the milk, salt, and sugar in the bowl of a heavy-duty electric mixer and add the sponge. Switch on at the lowest speed and work with the dough hook for 2 minutes. Turn up the speed slightly and work for 6 minutes, when the dough will be soft and sticky, and coming away from the sides of the bowl. Put the dough in a plastic bag and leave overnight in the refrigerator.

The next day, put a sheet of plastic wrap on the work surface and dredge with flour. Lay the butter, which should be firm but not hard from the fridge, on top. (If too soft, you will not be able to control it.) Sprinkle a little flour onto the butter and, with a rolling pin, bang it out into a rectangle about ½ inch thick. Wrap with the plastic wrap and place it in a cool part of the kitchen. (If the room is hot, return the butter to the refrigerator for a few minutes.)

Take the dough out of the bag and put it on a floured work surface. Deflate it with the rolling pin. Scatter more flour on top of the dough and on the rolling pin, then roll out, turning frequently, into a rectangle about ½ inch thick. Brush off any obvious flour, then put the unwrapped butter in the center. Fold the edges of the dough over the butter so that they slightly overlap at the top and the butter is completely enclosed.

Scatter some more flour over. Rolling always away from you, roll the dough out into a long rectangle about 16 x 26 inches. Fold one short end in by a sixth and then the other short end in by a sixth. Fold both ends over again by a sixth so that they meet in the center. Now fold the two together, as if you are closing a book. Turn the dough so the fold is to one side. Roll it out gently away from you again into a long rectangle about the same size as before. Fold one end of the dough in by a fourth and then the other end in by a fourth so that they meet in the middle. Now fold the two together, as if you are closing a book. Seal the edges with pressure from the rolling pin. Wrap in plastic wrap and refrigerate for 30 minutes to 1 hour.

Make a triangular template 7 x 7 x 6 inches from cardboard or rigid plastic. Roll out the dough on the floured surface to as neat a rectangle as you can, about 30 inches long, 12 inches across, and ³/₈ inch thick. Trim to give straight edges, then cut in half lengthwise. Using the template, mark out and cut 8 triangles from each piece of dough.

Lay the triangles, one at a time, on the lightly floured surface with the narrow point away from you. Roll up away from you, finishing with the point in the middle and underneath. Lay the croissants on large baking sheets lined with parchment paper, leaving space around them to allow for expansion. Cover with plastic wrap and let rise in a warm place until doubled in size, which should take 1–2 hours.

Preheat the oven to 400°F.

For the glaze, whisk the egg yolk and milk together. Brush lightly onto the croissants, brushing from the middle out so the glaze does not get between the dough layers—this could cause them to stick and would impair the uniform rise. Bake in two batches in the center of the oven for 10 minutes, when they will have expanded and started to color. Reduce the oven temperature to 300°F and bake for a further 20–25 minutes or until risen and golden brown. Cool on a wire rack, arranging the croissants so they are not touching.

Danish pastries

We use croissant dough for our Danish pastries because it gives a crisper and less doughy finish. The pastry can be cut into squares or rounds and baked in pans, or it can be shaped into coiled ropes. Pastry cream and fruit are traditional toppings. The baked pastries are glazed here with apricot jam, but you could also use a lemon icing (see Lemon cake, page 107).

MAKES 6 PASTRIES

10 OZ. (300 G) CROISSANT DOUGH (PAGE 148)
A SELECTION OF FRESH, CANNED, OR BOTTLED FRUIT, SUCH AS PEACHES OR NECTARINES, PLUMS, APRICOTS, APPLES, PEARS, FIGS, OR PASSION FRUIT FLESH, OR DRIED FRUIT, SUCH AS RAISINS, FIGS, CHERRIES, APRICOTS, AND CANDIED PEEL
ABOUT $^2/_3$ CUP (150 G) PASTRY CREAM (SEE CHESTNUT MILLE FEUILLES, PAGE 141)
LIGHT BROWN SUGAR FOR SPRINKLING (OPTIONAL)
FLOUR FOR ROLLING
3–4 TABLESPOONS APRICOT JAM

GLAZE
1 EGG YOLK
1 TABLESPOON MILK

If baking the pastries in pans, put six 3-inch fluted tartlet pans on a baking sheet and brush each inside lightly with oil.

On a floured work surface, roll the dough to $^3/_8$-inch thickness. Using a 4-inch round cutter (or a sharp knife), cut disks or squares from the dough and lay these in the tartlet pans. Press the dough lightly into the corners of the pans. Alternatively, shape the dough into thin ropes and coil around into 3-inch circles on baking sheets lined with nonstick baking liners or parchment paper. (At this point you can freeze the shaped dough for up to 1 week; thaw before rising.) Cover with plastic wrap and let rise in a warm place until doubled in size, which should take 1–2 hours.

Preheat the oven to 350°F.

If using fresh or preserved fruit, cut it into neat slices or dice, peeling as necessary. Dried fruit should be soaked briefly in hot water and then dried on a towel, unless it is very plump and moist.

For the glaze, whisk the egg yolk and milk together. Spoon 1–2 tablespoons of pastry cream into the center of each dough case, and spread the cream with the back of the spoon to cover the bottom evenly. Arrange the fruit on the pastry cream, fanning slices neatly or scattering on diced or small fruit. Sprinkle with brown sugar, if desired. Brush the exposed edges of the pastry case with the egg wash.

Bake for 35–45 minutes or until the pastry is risen and golden brown.

Warm the jam in a small pan until melted. Press it through a sieve to remove any large pieces of fruit, then brush over the warm pastries to glaze.

Danish pastries and
Pains au raisin, ready
for baking

Pain au raisin

Pain au raisin is really a grown-up sticky sweet roll, the dried fruit plumped in rum, the surface attractively glazed. Interestingly, during an experimental sub-contracted delivery program at Baker & Spice, it was always the boxes of pain au raisin that became mysteriously depleted somewhere between the bakery and the customers, giving credence to the phrase, "they are simply irresistible."

MAKES 6 PASTRIES

10 OZ. (300 G) CROISSANT
DOUGH (PAGE 148)
1²/3 CUPS (250 G) RAISINS,
SOAKED IN WARM WATER
FOR 30 MINUTES
1 TABLESPOON SUGAR
¹/2 TABLESPOON RUM
FLOUR FOR ROLLING
3 TABLESPOONS APRICOT JAM

GLAZE
1 EGG YOLK
1 TABLESPOON MILK

Line a baking sheet with a nonstick baking liner or parchment paper.

On a lightly floured surface, roll out the dough to a ³/8-inch-thick rectangle.

Drain the soaked fruit and put it in a bowl. Add the sugar and rum, and toss to coat. Spread evenly over the surface of the dough. Take one long edge of the dough rectangle and roll up like a jelly roll, taking care none of the fruit falls out. With a sharp knife, cut this cylinder into slices about 1 inch thick. Place them on the lined sheet, with space around them. (They can now be frozen for up to a week; thaw before rising.) Cover with plastic wrap and let rise in a warm place until doubled in size, which should take 1–2 hours.

Preheat the oven to 350°F.

For the glaze, whisk the egg yolk and milk together. Brush this over the pastries. Bake for 35–45 minutes or until risen and golden brown.

Warm the jam in a small pan until melted. Press it through a sieve to remove any large pieces of fruit, then brush over the warm pastries to glaze.

Choux paste

Choux is a pastry oddity, being part cooked prior to baking and—with its high egg and water content—presenting as a pipeable paste. During baking the water in the paste creates steam internally, encouraging the choux to expand rapidly and set as a crisp shell with a hollow center. This space can be filled with set custards, whipped cream, or savory mixtures.

Accurate measurement of the ingredients is important, though in this recipe the precise amount of egg is deliberately not specified. You need about one egg to each scant ¼ cup (30 g) of flour, but eggs vary in size and flours have different absorption levels. The thing to do is beat in 3 eggs sequentially and then beat in the fourth a little at a time, stopping when the mixture is the right consistency. If you don't put in sufficient egg, the paste will be too dry to expand; if you add too much the mix will be too sloppy to pipe.

1 CUP (150 G) ALL-PURPOSE FLOUR
3–4 EGGS
7 TABLESPOONS (100 G) UNSALTED BUTTER
1 TEASPOON SALT
1 CUP (250 ML) WATER

Sift the flour into a bowl. Have 3 eggs to hand, whisking the fourth to a liquid in a bowl and reserving.

Put the butter, salt, and water in a heavy-based pan and bring to a boil over a medium heat. As the water comes to the boil, remove from the heat and dump in the flour all at once. Immediately stir briskly with a wooden spoon until the flour and liquid are evenly combined.

Lower the heat and set the pan over it, beating continuously for a minute, when you will have a coherent mass that comes away easily from the side of the pan. Remove from the heat and let cool for about 3 minutes. (If you add the eggs immediately, the heat of the mixture may cook them, setting curds and ruining the texture.)

Beat the first 3 eggs into the mixture, one at a time, making sure each egg is completely incorporated before adding the next. The mixture should be smooth and glossy. If too stiff, trickle in some of the beaten fourth egg from the bowl, beating well, and continue adding egg until the pastry looks and feels right. It should hold to the spoon and only drop from it slowly.

Let cool to room temperature, then use immediately. If left to cool too long the choux paste will stiffen so that you will not be able to pipe it or spread it easily.

Mexican hats

The pastry puffs and lifts off the baking sheet as it bakes, forming an unusual shape. We call them Mexican hats, as they appear extravagantly brimmed, like a sombrero. Pairs of the crisp, airy disks can be filled with lightly whipped cream or pastry cream (see Chestnut mille feuilles, page 141), both perfect with seasonal berries.

MAKES 15 PAIRS OF CHOUX HATS

1 RECIPE CHOUX PASTE
(SEE OPPOSITE)
CONFECTIONERS' SUGAR FOR
DUSTING

Preheat the oven to 350°F. Take the largest, heavy baking sheet that will fit in your refrigerator and in the oven, making sure that it is spotlessly clean, and rub the sheet all over generously with soft butter. Refrigerate it for about 20 minutes.

Put the choux paste on the work surface next to the baking sheet. Put a spoonful of paste on the sheet and spread it with a metal or rubber spatula, starting at one edge, to make a rough round about 4 inches across and $^3/_8$ inch thick (1). Don't worry if it is a little uneven. The ripples made by the spatula will produce a more interesting hat. With your finger, trace a neat circle in the paste, cutting cleanly through to the sheet (2). Wipe any excess paste from your fingers. Spread another round of paste on the sheet, about $^3/_4$ inch from the first, and repeat until you have filled the sheet.

Place the baking sheet on the middle shelf of the oven and bake for 15 minutes, then reduce the temperature to 325°F and bake for a further 10–15 minutes or until the hats are puffed, lightly browned, and crisp. Lift the hats onto a wire rack to cool (3). Discard the choux trimmings left on the sheet.

Put the choux hats together in pairs with the chosen filling, and dust with confectioners' sugar before serving.

Éclairs

Of all the choux paste creations, éclairs are perhaps the best known and most widely enjoyed. With their crisp, light, and neutral-tasting shell, the contrastingly rich filling, and the shiny fondant icing on top, éclairs deliver a great deal for very little effort. They are easy to pipe, though it is a good idea to heat the knife or scissors you use to cut the paste as it extrudes, so the cut is clean and the sticky paste does not adhere to the blade. When the pastries come from the oven it is important to puncture them immediately, so internal steam does not soften the case. To be enjoyed at their best, they should be eaten as soon after they are filled and iced as possible.

If you have more fondant than you need for the éclairs, it will keep well in the refrigerator in a covered container.

MAKES 12–14 ÉCLAIRS

1 recipe Choux paste (page 152)
pastry cream (see Chestnut mille feuilles, page 141) or whipped cream for filling

FONDANT ICING
1 cup + 2 tablespoons (225 g) sugar
1/3 cup (75 ml) water
2 teaspoons liquid glucose or light corn syrup
2 tablespoons (15 g) grated bittersweet chocolate, or unsweetened cocoa powder to taste; or 1/2 tablespoon strong espresso
corn or sunflower oil for the slab

First make the fondant: put the sugar and water in a pan over a low heat and stir to dissolve the sugar. Add 1/2 teaspoon of the glucose (or a pinch of cream of tartar), then increase the heat and bring rapidly to a boil. Boil to the soft ball stage (235–240°F on a candy thermometer). Pour onto a lightly oiled marble slab and let cool for 3–4 minutes. (If you proceed while the sugar is too hot, the fondant will become grainy.) Working with a metal spatula or metal scraper, scrape under the mass, repeatedly scooping it up and over itself in a figure-of-eight movement. Continue working like this for about 10 minutes or until the mass becomes opaque and too stiff to lift with the spatula. Then start kneading with your hands, pressing and folding until the fondant is smooth and pliable. Form into a ball, wrap in plastic wrap, and refrigerate for at least 24 hours before using.

Preheat the oven to 400°F. Butter a baking sheet and chill in the refrigerator. Put a sharp knife or scissors in a pitcher and pour boiling water in to cover the blade.

Put the choux paste in a large pastry bag fitted with a 3/4-inch plain tip. Squeeze the bag down and twist the top until the first sign of paste extrudes, then pipe out onto the baking sheet in 4-inch lengths, cutting them with the hot knife or scissors. Leave space between the éclairs to allow for expansion.

Place the sheet on the middle shelf of the oven and bake for 15 minutes, when the éclairs will be well risen and have started to color. Reduce the oven temperature to 325°F and bake for a further 10–15 minutes or until the éclairs are lightly browned and crisp. Remove from the oven, immediately slit open to let any remaining steam escape, and transfer to a wire rack to cool.

Soften the fondant in a bowl set over simmering water. As it starts to soften, add the remaining liquid glucose. Add the chocolate, cocoa powder, or espresso while the fondant is being melted (or leave it plain if you prefer white icing). Remove from the heat and continue stirring until the icing coats the back of the spoon. The consistency should be like that of heavy cream.

Fill the éclairs with pastry cream or whipped cream, piping it into the slit. Hold each éclair upright over the bowl of fondant and spoon the icing on the top side, letting it run down to make an even layer. Let cool and set before serving.

Mexican hats and Éclairs

GLOSSARY

active dry yeast Commercially produced yeast, in granular form, made up of the living cells of the yeast strain *Saccharomyces cerevisiae*. When fresh, it is usually sold in small, moist, compressed cakes.

allspice Aromatic brown berry the size of a large peppercorn that is dried in the same way. In its complex aroma one can smell hints of mace, cinnamon, and cloves.

baguette Light-textured, long (about 30 inches) French loaf baked with soft white flour, which originated in Paris as late as 1920. It is characterized by a beautifully thick, crackling-crisp crust, but stales within hours.

baking powder Leavening agent, a mixture of baking soda and acid salts, that only needs moisture to activate it. Baking powder also contains a larger percentage of ground starch, which is included to absorb moisture from the air and prevent premature activation in the can. It is used with soft flour to make "quick" bread.

baking soda Leavening agent, more properly sodium acid bicarbonate. When baking soda, an alkali, is mixed with an acid, a chemical reaction is kick-started and carbon dioxide is given off.

banetton Linen-lined wicker basket, of different shapes and sizes, in which doughs are left to rise.

barm Leavening agent containing yeasts from the froth produced during beer fermentation.

beignet Deep-fried, yeasted bread dough. The name is interpreted differently in different parts of the world—it can be a plain doughnut or a fruit fritter.

beurre manié Paste made from equal parts of flour and butter,

also called kneaded butter, used mainly as a thickening agent.

biga Italian version of poolish, based on the high-gluten flour used for pastamaking.

bolting, boulting Successive sifting of flour to make whiter, refined flour.

bran Outer husk of wheat.

brioche Sweet yeasted bread enriched with butter and egg.

Callibaut Couverture Fine high-cocoa-content chocolate with a strong bittersweet taste.

choux (pastry) Pipeable, egg and flour paste used for making hollow cases such as éclairs and profiteroles (cream puffs).

cinnamon Dried inner bark of a tropical tree. Cinnamon is preferable bought as rolls or quills of bark rather than as a ground powder, because the latter rapidly loses flavor and aroma.

crème fraîche Rich French cream with a distinctive tangy taste. It is made from heavy cream mixed with buttermilk heated to a constant 170°F for several hours until it thickens and stabilizes.

crumpet Round, yeast-raised unsweetened bread. Crumpets are cooked as a batter in ring molds on a griddle, which produces a dark brown base and a pale top pocked with holes.

deflate Pressing risen dough to expel the carbon dioxide trapped as bubbles by the gluten.

éclair Long choux container usually filled with whipped cream or pastry cream.

ferment, fermentation Process during which carbon dioxide is given off. This is a result of yeasts producing alcohol as a byproduct of getting chemical energy from sugars.

ficelle White French loaf made in the same length as a baguette, but much thinner.

focaccia Rectangular yeasted white bread with a dimpled surface. The bread is dressed liberally with olive oil and sea salt just before it goes in the oven. It often has rosemary leaves on top, too.

fougasse Oval yeasted flat bread from Provence, France, distinguished by slashed holes cut through the loaf in a rough herringbone or leaf-on-the-branch pattern. It may be plain or filled.

gluten Combination of two proteins found in wheat grain, which, when moistened, bind together, creating thin, elastic strands. These form membranes that trap the gas, causing the dough to rise.

grissini Crisp bread sticks first made in Turin, Italy.

knead Working and mixing flour and water together to make a coherent, elastic, and pliable mass (dough). Kneading can either be done by hand or using an electric mixer fitted with a dough hook. The process encourages the gluten in flour to stretch and expand, and acquire the necessary elastic and plastic properties to trap gas bubbles given off during yeast fermentation (leavening, rising).

lemon zest Thin outermost layer of the rind. Zest is used in many recipes as it contains the volatile oils that deliver the most intensely lemon flavor. Unless organic, always scrub lemons thoroughly before removing the zest because of chemicals and the coating of antifungal wax, the latter having been applied to retard oxidization.

levain, leaven Dough colonized by airborne yeasts, which is used to raise sourdough breads.

mace See nutmeg.

meal Coarse flour.

miche Large, round French country loaf, usually a sourdough.

mille feuilles Multi-layered puff pastry confection. Literally "thousand leaves," this is not an accurate description as there are really 723.

muffin Small, sweet "quick" bread leavened with baking soda or baking powder.

nutmeg Seed of the fruit of *Myristica fragrans*, the tropical nutmeg tree, which originated in the Moluccas but is today cultivated in many tropical countries. The seed is covered with a reddish, fibrous membrane that separates it from the flesh of the fruit. When dried and flattened this membrane becomes mace. Mace and nutmeg smell and taste similar and are interchangeable, though mace is stronger in flavor.

oats Coarse cereal popular with horses and eaten by humans in oatmeal, granola, and oat cakes.

palmier Sugary cookie made from puff pastry.

pane bianco Classic Italian loaf baked with minor regional variations throughout Italy—their version of a French pain de campagne.

pastry cream Thick, flour-stabilized egg custard, also called *crème pâtissière*. Usually flavored with vanilla, it is an essential preparation in pastrymaking, being used to fill tarts and many other pastries.

peel Flat beechwood head attached to a long shaft, used for loading and unloading breads and pizzas from traditional ovens.

pithiviers Glazed, round puff pastry pie with a rich, sweet filling. Pithiviers is traditionally scored on the top in radiating curved lines.

polenta Meal ground from dried corn (cornmeal).

poolish Starter batter colonized by airborne yeasts, which is used to raise sourdough breads.

pretzel Loosely twisted knot of crisp white yeasted dough. The history of the pretzel can be traced back to Roman times, but they are today seen as American, because the first pretzel factory was established in Pennsylvania in 1861.

profiterole Small choux bun that may be filled with either sweet or savory creams. When sweet it is often called a cream puff.

punch down Overly aggressive technique to deflate dough after initial rising(s).

quick bread Bread raised using chemical leavening agents, such as cornbread, soda bread, scones, muffins, and biscuits.

rye Low-gluten cereal. When milled it produces a dark, heavy flour with a pronounced flavor.

semolina Durum wheat that is more coarsely ground than standard wheat flours.

soda bread Soft wheat-flour loaf usually leavened with baking soda; originally Irish.

sourdough Bread leavened using wild yeasts and given a distinctive sour tang from the lengthy fermentation involved.

sponge Preliminary flour, yeast, and water batter. Once active, the sponge is used to raise the subsequent dough.

spring water Purified bottled still water without chemicals.

sumac Red powder made from the dried berries of the shrub of the same name, which is used extensively in Iraqi cooking.

taux des cendres French designation of the level of bran in a flour, based on the ash left behind after the flour has been incinerated in a laboratory at 900°C.

vanilla bean Dried long, thin pod of the orchid *Vanilla planifolia*. The principal flavor resides in the seeds.

Viennoiserie French pâtisserie term for fine flaky pastries such as puff pastry and croissants, in which crisp layers result from the careful incorporation of butter during repeated rolling and chilling.

wheat germ Oily embryo of the wheat "berry" or kernel. Wheat germ is a concentrated source of proteins, vitamins, and minerals.

whole-wheat Flours darker in color because they are made using elements of the whole wheat berry, including some of the wheat germ and bran.

yeast Microscopic single-cell organism that produces alcohol and carbon dioxide as it grows, a process called fermentation. To do this it needs sugars, moisture, and warmth.

zahtar Mixture of equal amounts of powdered sumac and dried ground marjoram and thyme.

INDEX

ACKNOWLEDGMENTS

Baker & Spice
46 Walton Street
London SW3 1RB UK
www.bakerandspice.com

We have about 20 full-time staff working to create the food we make every day. Of course, this cast changes from time to time, but without the extreme hard work and dedication of our exceptional crew we would not be where we are today. The staff who have helped to create the shop we have today, listed chronologically, are:

For the bakery: David Frequelin, Remi Georgelin, DL, Amir Allon, Martin Aspinwall, Jason Warwick, Remek Sanetra, Henri Bellon de Chassy, Damon Cowan, Sally Parsons, Amar Slimani.

For the Viennoiserie: Patrick Lozach, Ram Sivaram, Martin Doak, Lionel Rocher, Ilan Schwartz, Mariangela Pratt.

For the pâtisserie: Henri Berthaud, Yannick, Amal Ibrahim, Ari Aboso, Alexandra Queruel, Yvan Cahour, Dorit Mainzer, Jeanne Hertz, Linda Osedo, Louise Riviere, Jaime Foa, Megan Jones, Mark Lazenby, Markus Herz, James Webb.

For the traiteur: Lorraine Dunne, Sammy Leopold Santos, DL, Michelle Wong, Kate Lewis, Sami Tamimi, Ruth Taylor Hunt, Pavel Kuzdak, Cayetano Lopez.

For the shop: Karen Copland, Natalie Laurent, Zoe Field, Tamsin Borlase, Anne Boyle, Fiona Kinnear, Stephane Boucton, Leonor Gomez, Laurent Beauvois, Helena Allon, Fabio Calascibetta, Alessandra Figini, Belen Mateo, Jaclyn Dove, Emma O'Reilly, Naima Ali, Anna Plym, Jenny Mellquist, Andrea Novak, Eric Ackermann, Daniel Marcolin, David Doulay, Candice Nieper, Kirsty McGregor, Amanda Hale, Anna-Marie Briers, Ari Economakis.

Kitchen assistants: Vince Mejia, Tito Bosales, Cesar Aristizabal.

For the bread factory and gail force: Amnon Mer, Pierre Corneille, Richard Vintiner, Samantha Oyez, Jackie Hobbs, Terry Stockwell, Nimal Kandihi.

Our drivers: David Ormston, Paul Stimson, Steve Bragg, Richard Fenton, Ray Mechell, Errol Palmer, Arthur Albert.

Our friends: Melanie Pini and Sophie Braimbridge (who suggested and created our first series of chef demonstrations), Naomi Kaplan (forever a source of inspiration), Anissa Helou, Peter Gordon, Jeremy Lee, Lyn Hall, Ursula Ferrigno, Giorgio Locatelli, Elizabeth Luard, Alastair Little, Juliet Peston, Heston Blumenthal, Jonathan Archer, John Kelly, Enzo Zaccharini, Honor Chapman, Sarah Standing, and the customers who have supported us from the beginning.

All our recipes have an origin, as do the recipes in every cookbook. Though these recipes have been written or adapted and tested by Dan Lepard and Richard Whittington especially for this book, the ingredients, techniques, and inspiration have come to us from our friends. Additional recipe credits are:
Dorit Mainzer for the Chocolate pecan cake, Devil's food cake, Marble cake, Lemon cake, Parmesan disks, and Chocolate chip cookies.
Naomi Kaplan for the Plum cake and Pecan butter cookies.
Jason Warwick for the basic levain and Roquefort and walnut fougasse.

For the production of this book, Baker & Spice would like to thank Divertimenti of Fulham, Kitchen Aid UK, Phillip Brittain and Solstice, Neal's Yard Dairy, Jeni Wright, Peter Howard, Coralie Bickford-Smith, Bridget Bodoano, and Caroline Perkins.

We would like to thank Emily Andersen for the use of her photographs on pages 7, 9, 10, 13, 14, 19, 20/21, 31, 35, 45, 49, 91, 93, 94/95, 102, 114/115, 129, and 138.

Baker & Spice breads (as well as a selection of British cheeses, olive oils, flour, and provisions) are available through Neal's Yard Dairy, mail order in UK mainland only (020 7407 1800).